iGod

iGod

A Hidden and Fragmentary Autobiography

Donald Wallenfang

WIPF & STOCK · Eugene, Oregon

IGOD
A Hidden and Fragmentary Autobiography

Copyright © 2021 Donald Wallenfang. All rights reserved. Except for brief quotations in critical publications or reviews, no part of this book may be reproduced in any manner without prior written permission from the publisher. Write: Permissions, Wipf and Stock Publishers, 199 W. 8th Ave., Suite 3, Eugene, OR 97401.

Wipf & Stock
An Imprint of Wipf and Stock Publishers
199 W. 8th Ave., Suite 3
Eugene, OR 97401

www.wipfandstock.com

PAPERBACK ISBN: 978-1-6667-0006-0
HARDCOVER ISBN: 978-1-6667-0007-7
EBOOK ISBN: 978-1-6667-0008-4

11/18/21

To the Most Holy Trinity—Father, Son, and Holy Spirit

O God, you are my God, for you I long;
for you my soul is thirsting. (Ps 63:2)

CONTENTS

Preface | ix

Chapter 1   Adopted from Kalamazoo | 1
Chapter 2   Do I Dare Disturb the Universe? | 29
Chapter 3   Bucket Full of Dreams | 59
Chapter 4   Crossroads | 85
Chapter 5   Grapevines | 118
Chapter 6   Playground of Life | 135
Chapter 7   Rendezvous with Destiny | 168

Bibliography | 209

PREFACE

IN MANY WAYS, THIS has been the easiest and yet most difficult book to write. Over the course of the past nine years, I have chipped away at this text, gathering up memories like ripe berries from a fruitful bush. Even as I write this final word that is at once the first word of the book, still during the trying season of the COVID-19 global pandemic, I am beset with trepidation and uncertainty. Will this book serve the purpose I have intended it to serve? Am I being too transparent with my life, too vulnerable? Will it, in the end, only contradict the message it hopes to convey—a definitive, indelible and irreversible conversion and inversion of "iGod"? I must place it all in the hands of the Lord, that this book, in some small way, might stir up at least a little more conversion in one of its unsuspecting readers.

It is slightly unnerving to complete an autobiographical book at a time of life that seems to be still in the middle, rather than at the end. But perhaps it is this acute sense of immanent end—an end that is always a beginning—that inspires this author to risk such a partial and precarious narrative. It is for you, the reader, that I write. I must share my story with you, even if we are virtually strangers, in order to testify to "what marvels the LORD worked for us" (Ps 126:3). "God, you have taught me from my youth; to this day I proclaim your wondrous deeds" (Ps 71:17). It may be that, when you read my story, people and places and events will light up from your own story all the more. It is necessary that we take time to remember a past become present, just as it is necessary that we not fail to trust in "a future filled with hope" (Jer 29:11).

As the subtitle of the book suggests, it is a hidden and fragmentary autobiography. This, I feel, is the only way I can tell my story and do some semblance of justice to all that will remain unsaid and even unremembered for now. Our lives are saturated phenomena, to be sure. Much more abides on the hindside of memory than those few fragments that come to the surface. Yet somehow those few fragments that come to the surface serve to recapitulate and witness to the whole constellation of life's meaning that is too wide to tell. The fragments of my life that I share herein are true. This is the way my life has unfolded, and I wish to tell it like it is. I do not want to obstruct the narrative by some pretentious academic discourse or pseudo-hagiography. I do not want my story to be told as a performance, but rather I simply want to put it on display in all of its sincere duplicity that yearns to undergo a metamorphosis toward sincere sincerity. I tell my story with full knowledge that it is not over. The conversion and inversion of "iGod" is still underway, and, I would like to hope, the apogee lingers around the eschatological corner of an untold rendezvous across an unexpected horizon of surprise and wonder.

This story is not so much about me as it is about my awesome God—Father, Son, and Holy Spirit—who has been at work every day and night of my life. He is the Reason for my story, the Melody of my song. I am his witness, or so I desire to be. May the words and photographs of this book point to him and not to me. "So this joy of mine has been made complete. He must increase; I must decrease" (John 3:29–30).

Donald Lee Wallenfang, OCDS / Emmanuel Mary of the Cross
September 24, 2020
Harsens Island, MI

CHAPTER 1

ADOPTED FROM KALAMAZOO

Memories risk being known rather than remembered.
—Emmanuel Levinas, 1986 interview with François Poirié

In the Ring

I HIT HIM—IN THE face. Right fist to left cheek—a perfect landing. All of the rage inside channeled through my shoulder, arm, and fist. Fight or flight. There was no way I was going to let a ten-year-old be victorious over me! Fight it was and my defining punch sent him flailing to the ground.

There we were, playing football in the Hamel's yard, right in the heart of our Higman Park neighborhood. My brother, Mike, had a friend over the night before and it was him and his friend against me and I don't remember who else. Somehow tempers started flaring and Mike's friend and I started getting into it. Pushing and pulling, twirling and shoving. Finally hitting. This was getting serious. Not the typical scene which resolves a couple seconds after it begins. Pride was at stake. Bam! Right in his face! Down he goes.

Bam! Right in my heart! Down I went—down to my knees in regret. As light snowflakes fell from the sky on that late fall afternoon, tears streamed down my face and apologies issued from my lips. "I'm sorry! I'm sorry! I'm so sorry!" I said this to him whom I slugged. I also looked up to heaven and said this to God. What I did was not right, this I knew without a doubt.

There was blood—maybe even a tooth knocked out (or so my memory wants to believe in its devilish pride). His mother came to pick him up. What have I done? What was the unrest in me which overflowed to my fist aimed at him, the other, the one who was not me and the one I sought to destroy—if even for a moment?

The Speed of Light

I envied my friend Josh. He had a ten-speed bike. Mine only had one speed. It was a thrill every time he let me ride it. This evening, we were all together—several of us friends in the neighborhood—and we decided to see who could ride around the Higman Park circle the fastest—on Josh's ten-speed bike. I would be the champion, no doubt. I was always the champion. One of the oldest kids in the pack, the perfectionist, always the "man of the moment," as my friend Brett once called me.

As we timed each of us, taking turns riding around the circle on Josh's ten-speed bike, I did come in with the fastest time: sixty seconds flat. No surprise. It was as if I owned his bike because I could ride it faster than him.

Later that evening, we were riding around the circle all together as we often liked to do. I remember talking with Josh specifically about our dreams. He was a smart kid. I remember asking him once that if he could have only one thing, and then be cut off from the rest of civilization, what would it be? He said, "A pencil and paper." I was like, "Why?!" He said, "Because I could write out my ideas." As we were riding around the circle this evening, I remember him saying that he hoped that when he got older, he would invent an object which could travel at the speed of light.

When Josh got older, he graduated from the Naval Academy and became a helicopter pilot for a while in the United States Navy. Following the unspeakably tragic 2004 tsunami, which claimed the lives of over 230,000 people, he delivered aid to the lands affected via helicopter—at the speed of love, the speed of light.

152 Higman Park—The home in which I was raised.

Uprooted

Growing up, my friend John and I were at times the best of friends, and, at other times, archenemies. We fought several times. Twice I remember punching him in the face, sending him home crying. Once I remember him pinning me down and choking me until I said "uncle" because I had been picking on one of the other neighbor kids. We must have become "blood brothers" a dozen times (as well as with all of the other boys in the neighborhood). Becoming "blood brothers" involved a ritual in which you put together bleeding wounds, signifying a kind of becoming family.

One day John and I were at each other again. I can't remember why, but I do remember that to retaliate, he uprooted several garden flowers which my Dad had planted outside our home and he strew them all over our yard. He even opened our front door and put one right in the middle of the entryway rug—dirt and all! I was so mad!

I marched over to tell him off to his face. I got to the front door of his house and he answered the door. I proceeded to yell at him with royal indignation. His mother came to the door and then slammed it in my face! I deserved it.

Morgan the Meatball

Bullying. An incredibly prevalent phenomenon among young people—and older people as well. Where does this diabolic surge to hurt others come from? There was a kid in our neighborhood named Morgan. He was a scrawny kid, a couple years younger than me, in my brother's grade. He played tennis and swam at the local country club, but he was also elusive on kick returns in our backyard football games!

Somehow, he acquired the taunting nickname, "Morgan the Meatball." I can't recall who came up with this sinister title for him. I hope it wasn't me.

I remember on one summer afternoon, several of us kids from Higman Park gathered outside his house chanting, "Morgan the Meatball! Morgan the Meatball! Morgan the Meatball!" I cannot remember what merited such derision, but surely it wasn't worth it.

Everybody's Everything

Growing up, there was a store in town called Everybody's Everything. It sold and rented out costumes. Perhaps it could be said that it symbolically empowered people to be who they were not. Masquerade.

At the end of first grade, there was an awards ceremony when all of the parents came to school and watched as their children received various awards from the first-grade teacher, Miss Mulherin. I remember anxiously watching all of the kids in my class receive their awards for various traits they exhibited throughout the year. Was I going to receive an award? Finally, at the very end, my name was called: Donald Wallenfang, "Most Outstanding Boy in All Areas." This was only the beginning.

In the living room of my Higman Park home, donning a Superman costume with a fireman's hat.

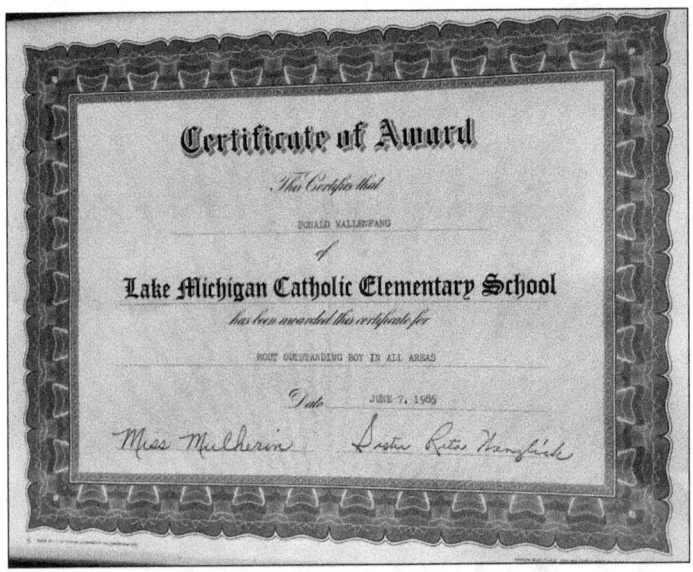

The certificate I received at the end of my
first-grade year from Miss Mulherin.

The Heartmenders

At the end of second grade I gave my teacher a hand-made gift certificate for free open heart surgery. I figured that by the time I became a fully licensed heart surgeon, she might be in need of some heart repairs. She was very grateful for the gift as it certainly warmed her heart. I wonder if she still has it to this day?

Later on, around the fourth grade, my brother and I played on a soccer team called the Heartmenders. I remember losing more games than we won—especially to our archrival: FOP, which stood for the Federal Order of Police. On one occasion, I was having (another) bad game and I got knocked down on the field toward the end. It kind of hurt, and I was given a free kick. Oh, how I wish I could have kicked that ball straight into the goal! Instead, I flubbed the kick and continued to cry on the field. After the game, I told my parents that my shoulder hurt really bad. They took me to a walk-in clinic, and I was diagnosed with "a pinched nerve." Rather, it was "a pinched ego," I think.

However, I do remember us winning a championship of some sort in which we played several games in a row one summer afternoon. I also vividly remember our team being treated to McDonalds food in between games. It was bliss at age eleven. At the end of the season, I also was awarded the George Herbert Walker award for most improved player. I still have the framed award in one of my many "special boxes" of keepsakes.

My father, brother, and I in our Heartmenders uniforms.

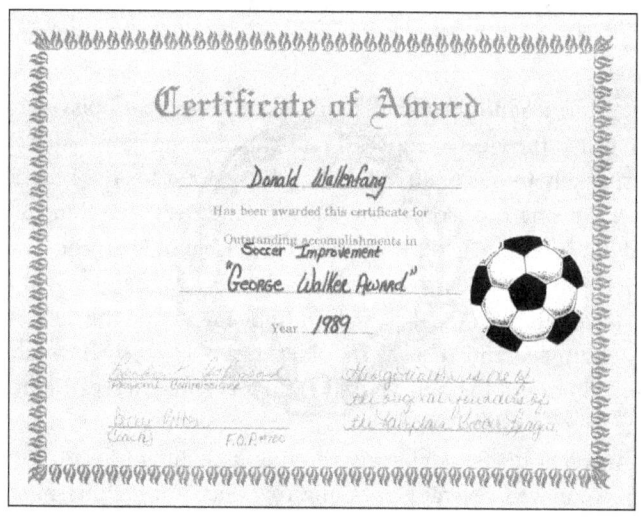

The award I received at the end of my 1989 soccer season with the Heartmenders.

Piggy Back

In Higman Park, there were two big hills with a neighborhood on each hill. I lived on Hill #1 and some of my friends lived on Hill #2. There was also a hilly trail, called Piggy Back, which ran between the two Hills. Piggy Back actually had two paths on it. One of the paths was higher and broader than the other. The lower path was narrow and sloped rather steeply in spots. My friends and I usually took the lower path, though adults would not dare. Occasionally we would inadvertently slide down the hillside in the process.

> I shall be telling this with a sigh
> Somewhere ages and ages hence:
> Two roads diverged in a wood, and I,
> I took the one less traveled by,
> And that has made all the difference.
>
> —Excerpt from *The Road Not Taken* by Robert Frost

I remember playing a game we called "War" often on Piggy Back and throughout the neighborhood. We would all get out our toy guns, hide, and then try to sneak up on each other and say "Ba-a-a-a-a-m!" It seems like no one ever won at this game, and yet it went on forever. We never tired of it and thought nothing wrong of it at the time.

Sam

Our good family friends, the Muldoons, had a black Labrador named Sam. I remember how he used to get so excited when we would come into the house. In the entry were the washing and drying machines, and Sam's tail would bang against them without stop.

As I got older, I was told by my parents that Sam used to guard my crib when I was a baby. He was a good dog. Memories of Sam are filled with such warmth and comfort. As Sam got older, he developed cataracts in his eyes. He became virtually blind, yet it didn't seem to slow him down any. It was as if he knew the neighborhood by heart, relying more surely on his other senses to get around. He was such a good dog.

Matchbox Car

Once when I was around seven years old, I was at my friend Nate's house playing with Matchbox cars. I enjoyed playing with those cars so much.

All of the different vehicle types and how you could create so many different scenes for them to play in. There was this one car which I coveted most of all. It was one of those fast sport cars that I hoped to drive in real-life when I got older.

When Nate wasn't looking, I pocketed the car. I remember leaving Nate's house that afternoon with such shame, guilt, and fear—like I was an escaped convict. The funny thing is that I don't even remember playing with that car at home. All I could think of was when and how I should return it to him.

On another day I went up to his front door and his mother answered. "This is Nate's car," I said. "I just wanted to give it back to him." I felt like I was baring the hell fires of my soul. I don't think she was able to see what was going on in my soul. Even at the age of seven, I knew what it was to steal.

Lord of the Rings

In Traverse City, Michigan, there is a resort destination called The Homestead. My family would go there with the Muldoons growing up. My parents were John and Linda, and I had only one brother, Mike. The Muldoon children were Creagon and Kaitlin, and their parents were Jim and Cynda. Jim and Cynda began an art and framing business, which they named Jamison Galleries, and my mom worked as its Vice President of Operations. My mom worked hard and she worked a lot. My dad had earned his PhD in political science from Purdue University and taught political science at Lake Michigan College in Benton Harbor, Michigan. My dad worked hard too, but he also liked to play!

We often would vacation with the Muldoons to different places and The Homestead was one of them. We went there a few winters to go downhill skiing. I remember Creagon teaching me the "tuck position" as the speed skiers like to do. I also remember going down the black diamond hills, some even with moguls. One winter, I went down the same black diamond hill twenty-five times in honor of Raghib "Rocket" Ismail, #25, of the University of Notre Dame football team. For I hoped to follow in his footsteps someday.

I remember seeing this girl around my age, maybe a little older, at The Homestead out on the slopes. Not that I ever said a word to her or even looked her in the eye, but I certainly had an affinity toward her. I only saw her in passing a handful of times, but it was enough for my imagination to run wild with childhood possibilities. Ahh—to be together.

Upon returning to school after this vacation around the sixth grade, I was showing off a colorful ring made out of woven string which I had acquired during the trip. I told all of my friends that this girl had given me the ring at The Homestead—the girl I never once talked to. I so much wanted to believe my lie, and I so much wanted my friends to believe it too.

Mousse

Around the third grade, we had grandparents' day at school. My Grandpa Lee and Grandma Ellen Wallenfang came in from Wisconsin for this special day. To make it even more special, my Mom helped me style my hair with mousse for the very first time—I was going to look sharp! Also, I was to wear a hand-me-down sweater for the first time.

However, a strange thing happened in the course of getting ready for school that morning. The mousse, which I had tried out the day before, had caused a severe facial rash! I had red spots all over my face and it was intense! How could I ever make it through the school day looking like this!

Finally at school, virtually everyone I came in contact with that day asked me, "What happened to your face?" My reply? "I got in a fight." There went the tough guy again. Not able to bear the embarrassment concerning the truth—was it really anything to be embarrassed about?—I was consistent about my lie. Perhaps I lied so much that I believed myself.

Cuddle Time

Growing up, I remember how much I loved "cuddle time" with my Mom and brother. Just about every night, the day would be ended with cuddling in my parents' bed, watching television. We would watch shows like *Diff'rent Strokes*, *Doogie Howser, M.D.*, *A Different World*, *The Wonder Years*, *Roseanne*, and *The Cosby Show*.

One of these nights, an unusual thing took place. For some reason, I had a panic attack. There I was, cuddling with my Mom and brother, and all of a sudden, I got on my knees in the bed and started praying out loud to God. "Please, Jesus! Help me, help me!" No one was sure what was going on. The next thing I know, my Mom was holding me and rocking me in the bathroom.

The experience of this panic attack led my parents to take me to the doctor, who then ordered various medical tests to try to determine what happened with me that night. I remember my parents thinking it had been some kind of seizure. At the hospital, I underwent an EKG, an EEG, and a CAT scan.

When I was about to undergo the CAT scan, I was injected with iodine. I had a severe allergic reaction to the iodine and started to go under in the hospital. I remember my vision and breathing being suddenly impaired. Thankfully the doctors and nurses were able to counteract the high amount of iodine and I ended up being okay.

"That's the Way It Goes"

I believe it was in the first grade. There my Grandpa Lee and Grandma Ellen were in town again, this time for Thanksgiving. All of the students in my class had to give short individual presentations which we had prepared on the theme of Thanksgiving. I had written a cute story about a turkey.

Though I don't remember exactly how the story went from beginning to end, I do remember how it ended. As any good Thanksgiving story would end, it ended with Thanksgiving dinner, which of course consisted of turkey as the centerpiece of the meal.

The story ended with this protagonist turkey losing its life to feed the hungry pilgrims. It ended with the words, "Well, that's the way it goes!"

Kalamazoo

I was born in Kalamazoo, Michigan, on February 24, 1978. My natural mother apparently had red hair and was into the arts. As I understand it, my natural father was a piano player and was married to another woman and had children with her. I was conceived through the course of an adulterous relationship—yet nonetheless conceived.

My natural mother lovingly gave birth to me on that winter day in 1978 and then gave me up for adoption through Catholic Family Services. She had requested that I be placed in a family who was serious about education, who loved music and sports, and who was Catholic. Her request was granted and, after living with a foster care family for six weeks, I was adopted by John and Linda Wallenfang of Benton Harbor, Michigan.

My adoptive parents were not able to have children naturally, so they decided to adopt. Two years after I was adopted, my brother, Michael, was born naturally of my parents on June 12, 1980. Without doubt, I was having a rendezvous with destiny.

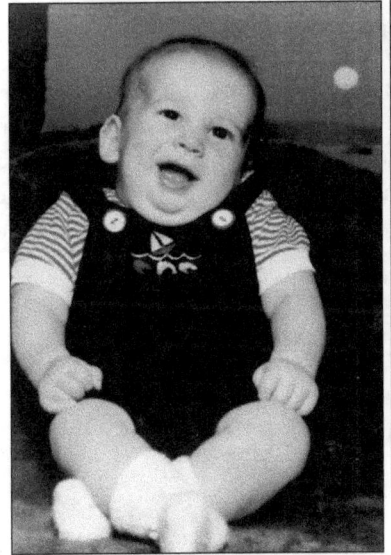

Pictures of my baptism and of different stages of childhood.
Note the number 3 appearing on my tank top at a very young age.

Water

Growing up in the Catholic Church and attending Catholic school until I graduated, my brother and I became altar servers. I saw serving as a privilege and I looked forward to it whenever it was our turn. There were older kids at my church who I looked up to and one of them was named Francisco Turner.

Fran was an all-American kind of kid. He was a straight-A student, tall, handsome, and a star athlete. He had a smile that ran all the way from the east to the west and everyone loved him. He and his brother, Daniel, were altar servers at my church and I wanted to be just like Fran when I got older.

Around the fifth grade, my brother and I were called to serve at the Confirmation liturgy with Bishop Donovan. He was an older bishop whose eyes sagged like those of a Saint Bernard, emanating an ancient wisdom and authority.

Right after the bishop anointed the confirmandi with the sacred chrism, it was time for him to wash his hands. My brother brought the basin and I brought the pitcher of water. A lemon also was used in the ritual hand washing in order to rinse the oil thoroughly from the bishop's hands.

Finally, it came time for me to pour the water over his hands to complete the ritual washing. I was trying to be careful not to overdo the water, so I poured what I thought to be just the right amount over his sacred hands. Looking me in the eyes with his eyes which seemed to hold the chambers of eternity, he said, "Don't be stingy." I proceeded to pour the rest of the water over his hands.

Fr. David Adams and I on the day of my First Holy Communion at Saint John the Evangelist Catholic Church in Benton Harbor, Michigan.

Dressed in altar server garb at Saint Anthony Catholic Church in Niagara, Wisconsin, the church of my baptism.

Numbers

I was one competitive kid growing up. I refused to settle for second place, even when I got second place. I was fiercely competitive, as if the whole world depended on it. Oftentimes my competitive nature would unleash itself on my younger brother, Mike.

There was no way Mike was going to oust me in anything—nothing. I internally vowed to be better than him at everything, and not only better than him, but the best in the world. For some reason, I believed that if his candle began to shine a little bit brighter than mine, all I had to do was blow his out. Thankfully, as I got older, I came across a saying which spoke to me directly: "Blowing out someone else's candle, won't make yours any brighter."

When I was in fifth grade and Mike was in third grade, we had a face-off in math. You see, Mike had Miss Ford for his third-grade teacher and Miss Ford didn't play around. She was the most feared teacher in the entire school, and her blue-gray eyes burned with fire. I did not have Miss Ford for my third-grade teacher, and I thanked God that my young life was spared.

Mike excelled in her class. In fact, he became the top math student that year. One day at school, I was summoned to Miss Ford's class to a math competition against my brother, Mike. In front of his whole class, we were to face-off on the same worksheet of multiplication problems.

Ready, set, go. Mike was lighting up his paper with brilliance while I floundered over basic equations. I even remember Miss Ford whispering to me the correct answers while my brother sped past the finish line with the greatest of ease. I was mortified. Perhaps I wasn't the best in the world at everything after all.

My brother, Mike, and I sitting on the branch of a tree along the shore of Lake Michigan where we grew up.

Sawed-off Shotgun

One night, around the fifth grade, I was lying on the living room floor doing homework and watching television. This was a typical evening scene at my home. Quiet, tranquil, pleasant, peaceful. There was much to enjoy, and enjoy we did.

Suddenly, my Mom came downstairs and told me to come upstairs right away. We lived on a bluff overlooking the shores of Lake Michigan. Not too shabby digs. Down at the beach, a little south of our home, was a public park called Jean Klock Park. My Mom alerted me that she had just heard a news report indicating that there was a man who had just robbed a gas station in Saint Joseph and was on the loose somewhere in Jean Klock Park with a sawed-off shotgun in hand.

My Dad was not home that evening as he was teaching a night class at Lake Michigan College. I panicked. I broke down in fear. What was a sawed-off shotgun, and who would want to saw off the end of their gun, anyway? I remember looking into the mirror, bawling my eyes out, saying, "I'm too young to die!" I don't even remember if my brother was home that night, though he must have been.

What would we do if he came to our house? I could see the police cars down at Jean Klock Park with their search lights. He never did come to our house, nor to anyone else's that I know. I believe he was captured by the police and arrested. He never made it to our house, but the fear did. Chicken.

Family Meeting

My brother, Dad, and I ate, drank, and breathed sports, especially football. Monday night, Thursday night, all weekend long the television was on with game after game, our eyes glued to it with the mesmerizing power of athletic valor. It seemed that the meaning of life was sports and winning the championship game.

My Mom was a workaholic. Every weeknight, I remember bringing in at least three bags and boxes from her company car so that she could work into the night. So, this was the scene at my house on weeknights: my Mom upstairs working in the home office, my Dad, brother, and I watching sports on television, my Dad occasionally grading papers at the dining room table, and, if we were lucky, making up a batch of popcorn.

One night, my Mom called a family meeting. Whenever we had a family meeting, everyone was all business. It meant that there was something serious to talk about together, and to resolve. For this meeting, my Mom had typed up a list of grievances against "the boys," that is, my Dad, my brother, and I. She threatened to leave if things didn't change.

One of her biggest complaints was that we were not keeping the house clean and tidy. I think my Mom may have had OCD before it was ever diagnosed as a disorder. My Mom would become infuriated at every little mess, especially if she found signs of our attempts at hiding the mess. One Saturday afternoon, I remember her charging at my brother and me with a belt! My brother and I would turn it all into a game, as if we were fleeing for our lives from a fire-breathing dragon! My Mom was not amused.

Things must have changed, at least somewhat. My Mom never ended up leaving, and we all seemed to get along better after that family meeting. Thank God for family meetings.

My Mom and I on the shore of Lake Michigan.
A sacred foot washing of sorts.

Pride and Prejudice

I grew up technically in the city of Benton Harbor, Michigan, which is demographically 90-percent African-American. However, in my neighborhood of Higman Park, there were no Black families to speak of. Higman Park was set on twin hills overlooking Lake Michigan and far removed from the Black community of Benton Harbor.

We would drive through Black neighborhoods just about every day and my perception of racial and economic difference was shaped over time. As one who wanted to be better than everyone at everything, race was just another differential which elevated me above others. I certainly had great African-American friends in school, on sports teams, and in music groups—and we got along just fine—but, generally speaking, I developed a sharp sense of prejudice against "Black people."

I gradually saw "them" as dirty, sassy, unsophisticated, and forlorn. I associated "them" with run-down houses, criminal activity, and Jheri curl. I viewed the natural distance between "them" and me as a healthy thing. Why couldn't "they" just get "their" act together and be like the rest of "us"?

Certain events worked to reinforce my ingrained perception of "Black folk." One summer evening, I was on my way to the beach with my brother, Mike, Creagon Muldoon, and Jim Muldoon. The Muldoons kept a catamaran on the shore of the beach throughout the summer. As we neared the edge of the bluff which overlooked the beach, we saw several African-American young people in the process of taking the catamaran out for a cruise.

Jim began to shout out at them, "Hey! Hey, what the hell are you doing?!" The young people immediately ran back to shore and took off running down the beach. We pulled the catamaran back into shore but felt shaken up by the experience.

On another occasion, my brother, Dad, and I were spending time at the beach one summer afternoon and there were a couple of Black boys about our age there next to us at our "private" beach. One of the boys began changing from his bathing suit back into other shorts right there on the beach. I looked on at him in disbelief. He looked back at me and snapped, "What are you looking at?! Are you gay?! Is your daddy gay too?!"

I was so angry at him that I wanted to fight. I felt like he had no business there on "our" beach, and to insult us besides? They eventually left, walking back down the beach to "their" side of town.

Much later in life, when my brother and I were in high school, I remember my parents asking us if we would be interested in partnering with an African-American kid or two in order to build relationships and help one another out. I immediately responded, "No way. I don't want anyone else to interfere with 'my' life!"

On the shore of Lake Michigan.

Nintendo

As I grew up, I became more and more entrenched in materialism. I fell in love with things—with possessing things—and I wanted more and more of them. Like the girl, Veruca, in *Willie Wonka and the Chocolate Factory* (1971), I wanted it all and I wanted it now. We would frequent the Orchard's Mall in Benton Harbor, and I would go crazy within. More clothes, more Air Jordan shoes, more toys, more candy. Anything and everything—give me more!

I literally worshipped things, that is, I gave ultimate worth and value to material possessions. I put my happiness in them and even when I read that someone shot someone else in order to steal away his Air Jordan's, I wasn't surprised. My lustful desire after things was murderous in nature. I would never hesitate to tear another apart with my words if it somehow would allow me miserably to rise above them in the sight of others.

As a child, Santa Claus was more than a god to me, for he was the supreme benefactor of stuff. At my upper/middle-class home, every Christmas he would bestow on my brother and me more gifts than we could remember. He seemed always to come up big with whatever we would ask for through the mediation of our parents. All we had to do was put out the milk and cookies for him at night and he would deliver the goods, except for one Christmas ...

It was the year 1986. The Nintendo Entertainment System (NES) was released on the market in North America just in time to begin begging Mom and Dad to get it for us for Christmas. My friend Brett ended up getting the new gaming system over the summer of that year—robot and all!—which only fueled my desire for it even more. This at last would make me happy!

Christmas morning came, and downstairs Mike and I rushed. I saw no boxes the size of an NES. We got to the end of opening gifts that morning and Santa left us with an epic fail. No NES. What's up, Santa?! We proceeded to leave later that morning for Green Bay, Wisconsin, where we would meet family and perhaps open the customary packages unveiling gloves and underwear.

As all was going rather uneventfully, our cousins Ryan and Danny were presented with a surprising package of promising size. They were given an entire fleet of Micro Machines from our Grandpa Dick! Mike and I were stunned, yet hopeful. How we wished that we would have just opened that package—but was there something else awaiting us? Something even better?!

The suspense rose until—yes, there was something else for us and it was just the right size!! We ripped through the wrapping paper, mixed with delight and greed, and behold—the Nintendo god! Could it be true?! Yes, yes, yes! And thus began an addiction.

ADOPTED FROM KALAMAZOO 21

My brother, Mike, and I opening our coveted
Christmas gift from Grandpa Dick.

The Golden Dome

In 1989, the University of Notre Dame football team defeated West Virginia University's squad to clinch the National Championship title under the leadership of coach Lou Holtz. With a perfect 12-0 record, Notre Dame was teaching an eleven year old in Benton Harbor what the true meaning of life was: perfection.

Situated roughly forty minutes north of South Bend, I was no stranger to the glitter of the golden dome. In fact, it bedazzled me. I was held spellbound by its magic. Notre Dame became for me the golden standard of perfection. It symbolized everything worth anything. Academic excellence. Athletic superiority. A monopoly on God. It was a grand synthesis of all that I knew of greatness. It even seemed to transcend God.

Virtually all of the valedictorians from my high school chose to go to school there. It was the land of the perfect—a promised land without blemish. Not a waking moment went by without me thinking of this destination in some way. Notre Dame was my paradise and my destiny—and I made sure to let everyone I knew know that.

I remember countless conversations with my Mom and Dad, always trying to convince them that not only could I play quarterback at Notre Dame, I was without doubt going to do so. Eventually, I was going to don the #3 jersey and follow in the line of all the greats: Ralph Guglielmi, Daryle Lamonica, Joe Montana, Rick Mirer, Ron Powlus. I was next in line. I grasped at this dream as if my life—and the world—orbited around its fulfillment.

Basking beneath the rays of the renowned Golden Dome on the campus of the University of Notre Dame.

Sporting the Notre Dame sweatshirt given to me by Msgr. Carl Steiner, the priest who baptized me.

Dropping back for a pass during a high school football game.

Shoot It

In seventh and eighth grades, I played football and basketball for the Lake Michigan Catholic Lakers. We were raggedy teams which tended to get beat by all the other schools. In seventh grade, our football team won only one game, and in eighth grade we won zero games. We got used to being the underdog and staying the underdog. I remember warming up for middle-school basketball games, looking across the court and seeing that the boys on the other team had facial hair! Some of them even had full beards! The opposing teams always seemed to be bigger and taller than us.

In such a perpetual underdog situation, you begin to develop a complex. You internally vow someday and somehow to overcome the odds and rise to the top. You swear to yourself that you will break the cycle of losing and gradually work your way into the winning circle.

This was something I swore to myself daily and yet found myself unable to risk all that needed to be risked in order to rise up. I often would refuse to try my best out of the fear that my best still would not be good enough. Out on the basketball court, I would refuse to shoot the ball because I was afraid to miss. If I didn't shoot the ball, I at least could keep telling myself that I would have made all the shots I didn't take.

Beaming with joy upon receiving the perfect Michael Jordan signature basketball as a gift.

Missing

One fateful winter night, I had played in a ninth-grade basketball game which was especially disheartening. I think I must have attempted some shots and missed them. Ninth grade was my most difficult year in school. I felt like I was at the bottom of the totem pole, which included experiences of being bullied by peers and coaches, very low levels of self-esteem, and dreams of greatness which never seemed to get off the ground.

After this particular basketball game, I deliberately avoided seeing my parents because I felt I had nothing to be proud of. I just wanted to avoid everyone in general. Around that time someone had told me that I often acted like a turtle. I would regularly "hide under my shell" and close off from the world. Instead of riding home with my parents after this game, or staying to watch the Junior Varsity or Varsity games, I decided to walk home by myself—through Benton Harbor.

I felt like I wanted to put myself in harm's way. I felt like I wasn't measuring up to anyone's standards of excellence—especially not my own—and I just wanted to get away from it all. I did this symbolically by treading through a rougher section of town, confronting my self-loathing with the cold night that enveloped me.

I remember walking across the bridge over the Saint Joseph river, which was near the county jail. I looked over the bridge at the freezing water below, wishing that it could painlessly swallow me in some sort of twisted loving embrace. Yet I kept walking toward the dream which sustained me.

I had no further encounters of note except for one. I walked by a billboard for WNDU News out of South Bend. It featured pictures of a few of their newscasters, one of whom was the sports newscaster. This station covered Notre Dame football like no other and reminded me of my destiny. "Jeff Jeffers would be announcing my name as the starting quarterback of the Fighting Irish in just a few years," I thought.

When I returned home, my Mom was sitting in a LazyBoy chair in the living room. She was sitting all alone in the dark crying. She had been worried about me. Shortly after this episode, I was taken to a counseling center to meet regularly with a psychologist.

Storm

At first, I was entirely reluctant to meet with a counselor. I was self-sufficient and didn't need any outside help. After a while, though, I ended up looking forward to these meetings because I could pour my heart out to this guy. He was a good listener and asked a lot of good questions which got me talking.

At one point, I remember telling him that I was the best at everything. It was as if I was barfing up all of the egotistical yuck that was in my heart. It allowed me to begin to get it all out of my system in a non-judgmental way. He would listen and ask follow-up questions, helping me to seek true perfection and not a cheap imitation.

During one of our counseling sessions, he asked me to look at two different pictures which were hanging on his office wall. The first was a serene scene of a warm and cozy cabin beside a river in the woods. There was a glowing sunset and the painting radiated tranquility and ease. The second image was one of a violent storm stirring through an open field in the countryside. He asked me which picture I would rather be in. The choice was easy for me—a no-brainer. Of course I would rather be in the still and peaceful one. He then told me that he would rather be in the one with the storm because it was more adventurous, exhilarating, and full of surprise.

I was dumbfounded. How could anyone in their right mind say such a thing?! Who would rather be in the middle of a storm than removed from such disruptive and menacing phenomena? Over time, though, I began to understand what he meant, and I would come to value life within the storm.

Mrs. Marty

There are those teachers in life who emanate the sheer goodness of learning and intellectual growth. Mrs. Marty was one of them for me. She was my English teacher for ninth and tenth grades. She was a no-nonsense kind of lady. Her dark blue eyes would penetrate right into your soul as she radiated a wisdom more ancient than time. Her décor was something out of the early twentieth century with ruffled blouses and hair that didn't move.

Mrs. Marty had a passion for literature and she conducted her class as if the world depended on it. She so much enjoyed teaching and energized learning according to her sustained fervor. There was not an assignment that went by which I did not complete for that class, even small and insignificant ones. Though scared to death in her class, it somehow empowered me to discipline myself in my studies. She helped to ingrain in me a work ethic which I would continue to develop into the future.

Ain't Misbehavin'

My Grandma Ellen was an exceptional pianist. She taught piano lessons throughout her life and played at many venues, such as parties and churches. In the fifth grade, I began playing the trumpet.

Eventually my Grandma and I played many songs together, especially enjoying jazz music, such as the classic 1929 tune, "Ain't Misbehavin.'"

It was a fun song to play, full of blues and sass. Yet it wasn't until much later in life when I realized the profound message of this song. The lyrics speak of the solitude and soberness of the lover, saving his love for his beloved, as well as the certainty of this love.

Are the words of this song not the essence of virginity? On several occasions, my Grandma and I performed our music in public. Another favorite tune of ours was the 1959 tune, "Edelweiss," from *The Sound of Music*. Never was there a time when I would not bring my trumpet when we went to visit her and Grandpa Lee in Niagara, Wisconsin.

Playing the trumpet with my Grandma Ellen Wallenfang at the piano.

CHAPTER 2

DO I DARE DISTURB THE UNIVERSE?

Hurdles

FRESHMAN YEAR OF HIGH school was the toughest of all. Arrested in puberty—that precarious time between childhood and adulthood—all I could do to hold myself together was dream. Football quickly became my life's meaning, and I realized how much work I had to do to achieve my lofty dreams.

I ran for the track team that year and somehow got stuck competing in the 300-meter hurdles. There I was, a scrawny 120-pound (if that) kid who wanted to come in first place every time, but instead found himself in last place—every time.

I wanted so bad to impress everyone. I wanted so bad to be affirmed as a great athlete. Yet I was so far from these accolades which I coveted so dearly. Fran Turner ended up being the State Champion in the 110-meter high hurdles his senior year of high school, even overcoming a severe hamstring injury that kept him out most of the season.

I was light years away from being a State Champion, but I never stopped seeing myself as a champion in the making.

"Milk, It Does a Body Good"

As a scrawny freshman, I was typically shy, but I also had my moments of boldness. One of them came during the summer on Silver Beach in Saint Joseph, Michigan. This was where all the babes hung out.

My friends and I were taking a break from our two-a-day football practices and went down to the beach to take a dip in the water. While we were there, we spied three older high school girls who we didn't know but who certainly caught our attention! How does one begin conversation in such a situation of inequality, fear, and trembling?!

I was suddenly inspired. I had it! Around that time there were these commercials for milk which gave the weakest of us hope. They portrayed a young skinny kid drinking milk and then growing up to be a strapping muscular young adult man. The message of the commercials was, "Milk, it does a body good." At the end of the commercial, the young man is shown walking happily away with his beautiful girlfriend. Needless to say, I drank a lot of milk my freshman year of high school!

I told my friend, Steve, of my plan. So, I went up to these young women as they were lying peacefully on their beach towels in their bikinis, while I was clad only in my bathing suit, and said, "Hey, ladies. I know that I look only like a scrawny little kid right now, but I'm drinking milk. And when I get older, I am gonna be one ripped dude, even more handsome than I am now," at the same time posing and making my muscles look as big as they could be.

One of the girls, the leader of the pack, immediately told me to go away, perhaps with some other explicatives added to her order. My friends were amused and thrilled, and my courage gained me not only hope, but the affirmation of my friends as well that afternoon.

Joining the Lake Michigan Catholic Lakers pep band for our halftime performance.

Do I Dare Disturb the Universe?

While in Mrs. Marty's freshman English class, I read the book, *The Chocolate War*, by Robert Cormier. I was struck by the underdog character, Jerry Renault, and his refusal to give in to The Vigils, a gang of boys which was trying to bully him. The book relates a poster that Jerry hung in his school locker on which was written this question: "Do I dare disturb the universe?" In the midst of being threatened, Jerry answered yes to this defining question.

I, too, took this question quite seriously, so much so that I made my own poster with a starry night sky, posing the question on a piece of masking tape: "Do I dare disturb the universe?" Like Jerry, I answered yes to this weighty question and attempted to march to the beat of a different drummer.

Marching to the beat of a different drummer at a young age.

Hand-off

The scene at school is ambivalent. One minute you feel embraced by the world and the next you feel lower than the sewer lines. Especially if you stand out in any way, someone is always right there to put you in your place.

As a freshman in high school, I was different. My Mom told me that I "marched to the beat of a different drummer." She was right. On dress-up days in school, I would where this tuxedo shirt with an artsy picture of a person with a top hat on the front of it. I got good grades and began to excel more and more in music.

I was back-up quarterback to a senior on our varsity football team, and I, too, endured all the hazing that is typical for freshman boys. On one occasion, I remember being lured into the varsity locker room after practice, only to have dirty poop-stained underwear put over my head. The senior guys called me "Wonny Dallenfang" (switching the letters of my first and last name) and never let me forget that they were the seniors and I was the freshman.

At the first varsity football game of the season, we were playing the Watervliet Panthers at their stadium. As usual, we began to get behind in the game. I stood on the sideline with my other freshman friends who were not expecting to play in the game, when all of a sudden I hear, "Donny! Donny! Get over here!"

Our senior quarterback had gotten injured and I had to go in as the backup quarterback! My heart had never pounded so fast in my life! The first play called was a safe handoff to the running back. "Blue 88! Blue 88! Set, hut!"

I successfully handed the ball off and carried out my fake with utmost precision. And there he went—thirty yards for the touchdown! My very first play in varsity football—a touchdown! I was famous in our school instantly. The senior quarterback was livid! He came back running on the field for the two-point conversion: "Wonny! Get out!"

> Writing a Journal Entry   10/30/92
>
> ### Game Day
>
> As I awoke on that memorable morning of October 3, 1992, I felt chills running through my body when I remembered that I would be playing quarterback for the Varsity football team that night. For the entire day I was breathing uneasily and my thoughts were focused entirely on football. I watched Rick Mirer and Notre Dame that afternoon so I could study his technique with undivided concentration and attention. My adrenaline was at its maximum level. I couldn't wait for the game to get under way. After arriving at our home field, Dickinson Stadium, I felt like I was the man of the moment. It usually doesn't happen that a freshman is able to start at quarterback in a Varsity football game. I was so excited and adrenalized. I can't explain the emotions I felt in words. I felt as if I were a knight in shining armor. I wanted to win more than anything in the world. I wanted to be just like Rick Mirer.
>
> Tomray #3
> Whelanfang

A journal entry remembering the day of my debut as the starting quarterback of the Lake Michigan Catholic Lakers varsity football team as a freshman.

In front of my Higman Park home on the night before the first varsity football game that I started as a freshman, versus the Berrien Springs Shamrocks. When this picture was developed originally, a different picture from another game was superimposed accidentally on top of it. I can be seen wearing a number 5 jersey that I used during our away games my freshman year.

Stupefyin' Jones

When I was a freshman in high school, I recall going to see the musical *Li'l Abner* at Saint Joseph High School. A female student played the part of Stupefyin' Jones, a statuesque woman who made the male characters freeze in their tracks as she walked by. This girl was the epitome of popularity and teenage beauty.

After seeing this show, I proceeded to tell the entire football team that I had a date with this girl (though I had never said a word to her in my life). At first, everyone thought I was making up the story. However, as I continued to insist that I had a date with her, they started to believe me. I talked about it so much that I think I started to believe me too.

Since I had formed this alleged alliance with Miss Popularity at Saint Joseph High School, I ascended to the ranks of popularity and acceptance at my own high school. At the same time, due to the suspension of the senior quarterback, I was slated to be the starting quarterback for the next Varsity football game, as a freshman! I was invited by none other than Francisco Turner to a Friday-night party where all the seniors would be. I was in!

As Fransisco Turner, another senior, and I were driving to the party, they were asking me about my date with this girl. At this point I had let my guard down because I thought I was finally in the in-group. I told them the truth: I had been making it up all along. The guy who was sitting in the back seat of the car said, "Not cool, man. Not cool." Once again, my ego sank back down to ground zero.

Collision

One night, my Dad, brother, his friend Kurt, and I were driving home from a girls basketball game in the country town of Marcellus, Michigan. I was driving our family mini-van and my Dad was riding in the front passenger seat while Mike and Kurt were riding in the very back seat. It was pitch black outside, and we were traveling down a country road at about fifty-five miles per hour. We had on a cassette tape of Georges Bizet's opera, *Carmen*, which my youth orchestra was practicing at that time.

All of a sudden, a deer darted out in front of our van and I had no time to slow down. We hit the deer head on and its antlers swung around and broke the front passenger window where my Dad was sitting! After hitting the deer, I brought the van to a stop on the side of the road. Everyone was okay, except for the deer.

The deer had died, and it was lying on the side of the road. An eight-point buck! We were not hunters in my family, so we did not keep the deer carcass. My Dad drove the van all the way home and all of us were a little stunned, but very thankful that nothing worse had transpired. When I told all of my buddies at school what had happened, the biggest question they asked was, "Why didn't you keep the deer?" Having more astute hunting sensibilities than me, they realized the value of an eight-point buck.

Sitting on Thin Air

Our Varsity football team won zero games my freshman year. By the time I was a sophomore, I was the starting quarterback of the Varsity football team, #3. Our uniforms looked identical to those of Notre Dame: gold helmets, Navy blue jerseys, gold pants.

Running out of the tunnel at Dickinson Stadium
where we played our home games.

This was it. This was my time to shine. Yet the hazing continued. The senior class that year had a couple bully kind of kids. In an instant they could sap the life out of you with what came out of their mouths.

I remember the scene of the school cafeteria. Whenever I walked across the room, it felt like everyone was watching me—especially on game days when we would wear our football jerseys over our school uniforms. Man, did we look sharp!

On one such Friday afternoon in the school cafeteria, I just didn't see it coming. I took my lunch tray up to the washing counter and returned to my seat. I was sitting with a bunch of seniors and felt quite high and mighty. As I was returning to my seat, it really seemed like everyone was watching me. I knew what they were thinking, "There he goes. The man. Donny Wallenfang, #3, quarterback of the LMC Lakers. Future quarterback of the Notre Dame Fighting Irish."

I neared my throne amidst the assembly of elders. They all seemed to be waiting for me with great expectation and admiration. There I went down to sit and continue to permit them to gaze on me with wonder. The problem was, when I went to sit down, there was only thin air! Down I went with the entire cafeteria population in hysterics!

One of my senior colleagues had pulled the chair out from under me! The classic prank. Down to the floor I crashed, not only my body but my soul too.

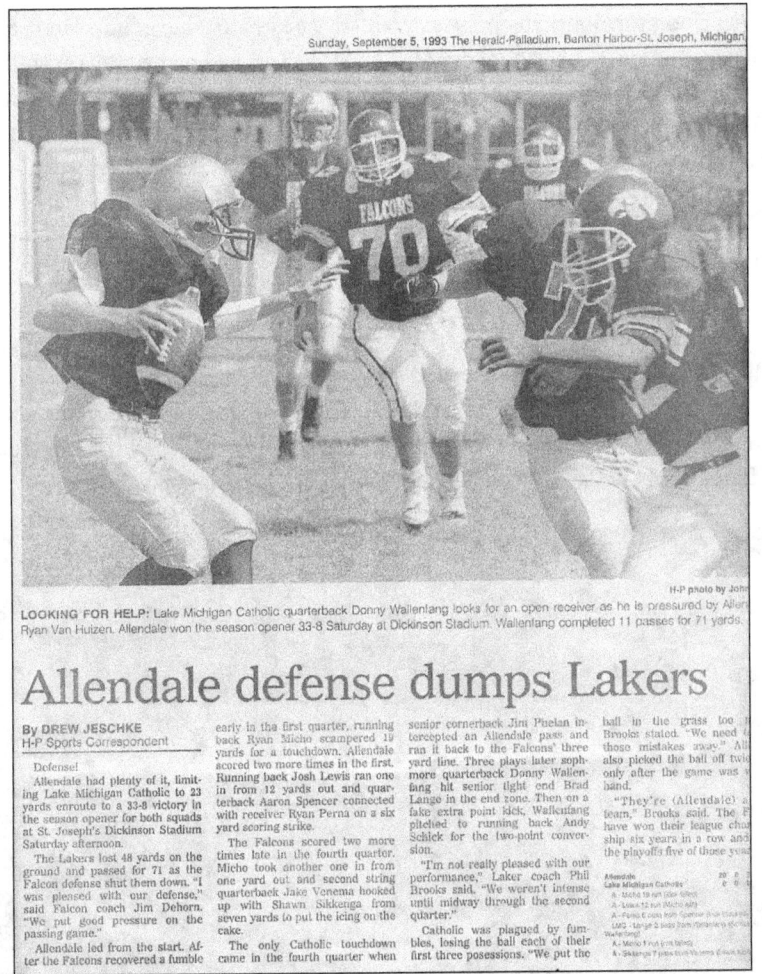

A newspaper article recounting our game against the Allendale Falcons during my sophomore year of high school.

Hot Wheels

When I was in eighth grade, I remember sitting in the dentist's chair and my dentist asking me what kind of car I would drive when I turned sixteen.

I told him, without missing a beat, that I would drive a Mercedes Benz. He had laughed at the seemingly unrealistic possibility. I really didn't know at that time what kind of car I would drive when I turned sixteen but could think of nothing less than the best.

Upon turning sixteen, I was granted the keys to a burgundy Mercedes Benz—though a 1979 300D model. The Muldoons had owned the car, and it was to become mine. It had leather interior, silver trim, and a diesel engine that hummed like a purring cat. It became the cause of simultaneous envy and admiration at school.

In addition, one of my brother's friends installed a twelve-inch subwoofer box that sat in the back seat. The Muldoons also generously updated the sound system to a detachable-face Pioneer tape deck and radio. I was rollin' to Shaggy's "Mr. Boombastic"!

Around this time, I gained not a little following of female students in the junior high. They even started a "Donny Wallenfang Fan Club," and all wore pins with my picture on them religiously. By this time, it became clear to all—I was the man—at least within the small universe which ran from Higman Park to Lake Michigan Catholic School and back again.

Creagon Muldoon and I tooling around in his father's Austin Healey.

Wise Fool, Part I

The word "sophomore" derives from two Greek words: *sophia* ("wisdom") and *moros* ("foolish"). This is indeed a fitting term for students in their second year of high school—not exactly immature any longer, but not quite mature either.

During my sophomore year of high school, I acted in many ways that would fit the definition. For example, I told a fellow football teammate that I could pass for over four-hundred yards against our defense. After that comment, I don't think that my offensive linemen blocked for me as well as before. On another occasion, during a girls basketball playoff game, I flatulated with such a stench right in the middle of the student body section of the bleachers that my peers hurled objects, limbs, and explicatives in my direction with great force.

Another instance I remember was during our high school band concert in the Mendel Center at Lake Michigan College. It was a beautiful venue to play a concert in the main auditorium. There was our band, dressed to the hilt and about to play the 1950's love song, "Only You," by the Platters. I had the featured trumpet solo for this song, but there was only one problem: my mouth was so dry that I could hardly get out a note! What to do?!

As our conductor, Mr. Jarvie, was introducing the piece, I went up to him in the middle of the stage and told him that I needed to get a drink of water because my mouth was so dry! My mouth got dry when I was nervous. He whispered, "Go ahead," and I ran out to search for the nearest water fountain. Finally, I found one and returned to play the solo with exquisite perfection. After that incident, I never performed on the trumpet without a glass of water on hand!

Performing on the trumpet at the Steeno home for a Wallenfang family Christmas jam session, and at Dickinson Stadium for a halftime show.

Intercepted

A quarterback's worst fear is being intercepted. It is the worst feeling on the field, even worse than getting sacked. While playing high school football, I threw more than my fair share of interceptions. Oftentimes they were the result of a desperation heave downfield, hoping that someone in the same color jersey as me would catch my pass sailing on a hope and a prayer.

Looking for an open receiver during our contest against the Allendale Falcons in 1993.

During my sophomore year, I threw four interceptions against the Galien Gales. I think I actually threw five interceptions, but one of them was called back for a roughing-the-passer penalty. I also was sacked a fair amount and one game against the Hartford Indians, I was sacked around a dozen times, most often by All-State linebacker, Steve Ackerman. After that game one of our fans described me as "Timex: He takes a lickin' but keeps on tickin'!" My Mom was not impressed.

Throwing interceptions wasn't something that stayed on the field. It seemed to follow you wherever you go. One morning at school, after a game against the Watervliet Panthers, I was walking down the hall courageously when I heard one student describing my performance during last Friday's contest: "Ya, his first two passes were for touchdowns! The problem was that they were touchdowns for the other team!" He was right, my first two passes of that game were intercepted and ran back for touchdowns.

In spite of my less-than-stellar performances on the football field, I had confidence that I was improving my game and had no doubt that I would one day run down the tunnel at Notre Dame Stadium, leading the Fighting Irish on to Victory.

Striking the Heisman Trophy pose for the camera
in a pair of plyometric training shoes.

Rudy

In the throes of my dreams, on October 13, 1993, a new film was released which helped to confirm my manifest destiny: *Rudy*. This film was on the serendipitous life of Daniel "Rudy" Ruetigger, who was a walk-on for the Notre Dame squad in the 1970s as an undersized athlete. His story is one of the underdog.

This was me too. I saw the story of Rudy as a kind of Old Testament to the New Testament which would be inaugurated by the manifestation of Wallenfang, #3. For me, it was a religious program and I put all of my eggs, so to speak, in this one basket of dreams. This dream consumed me, so much so that I said to my Mom in the kitchen one afternoon, "Mom, Notre

Dame is God; God is Notre Dame!" Everything hinged on the fulfillment of my self-prophecy. Yet, after I said this, my Mom encouraged me to pray more to God about his will for my life.

Even one of the cheerleaders' mothers made a Notre Dame sweatshirt for me with the ND insignia on the front and the #3 on one of the sleeves. I wore this sweatshirt to the opening of the move, *Rudy*, and other families from my school were in attendance as well. The stars were aligned and all that was left for me to do was to enter upon my cue.

Outside one of my relative's homes, wearing the sweatshirt made for me by a family friend in high school.

Fields of Gold

Also, around this time there was a song published by Sting called "Fields of Gold" (1993), which I found very meaningful. The lyrics tell of the contentment of a faithful and fruitful relationship that bears children, with constant reference to the calming sun shining on fields of gold. The song presents life as a unified and coherent constellation of meaning that the contemplative is able to recollect as gift.

Obviously for me it had the underlying imagery of the golden dome at Notre Dame, the golden helmets, and the football field. Yet its romantic meaning also resonated deep within my bones: Who was this mysterious woman? All my life I wondered who I would marry. This song spoke to me of my future bride who I had not yet met. This song lifted my soul in such a way that it made both future and past present.

Shoestrings

Growing up, my Dad was always there for me. I can't think of a greater gift to have as a young boy. He loved music, sports and academics. He could usually be seen at home grading papers or reading a book about political science while one of Beethoven's symphonies was playing in the background. He also frequently could be seen cooking in the kitchen or peeling potatoes while watching a football game on TV.

Yet never do I remember a time when my Dad said no to my request to come outside and play catch with me. It seemed like it was always yes. I have many memories of him setting aside what he was doing, grabbing his tennis shoes, sitting down on the couch and tying his shoestrings.

This was always a great gift to me. Then followed the bliss of throwing the football together in the front yard. Sheer joy.

Simultaneous kisses from my mother and father in our home as a young child.

Sunsets

Though my Mom worked day and night, keeping the books up-to-date for the art gallery, she, too, was always there for me. She and my Dad would come to virtually all of my athletic events, music performances, and honor roll banquets. They took great joy in the successes of Mike and me. It was as if our achievements were their achievements.

Many evenings, my Mom and I would sit and visit after our family supper. Our dining room featured a large window which looked out over a wooded bluff and over Lake Michigan. My Mom and I would have so many meaningful conversations, talking about life and dreams and even God. I recall the great warmth of these conversations as the sun went down for the night over the water. There was much love in the house.

My mother and father pictured on a ferry boat.

Reeperbahn

In the summertime, I often would attend Blue Lake Fine Arts Camp, a summer music camp about two hours north of where I grew up. I very much enjoyed these experiences, meeting new friends, playing great music, and telling hilarious jokes. In the summer of 1993, I auditioned for an international band through Blue Lake and was accepted to travel to Germany and Belgium the following summer.

Warming up my trumpet before an audition at
Blue Lake Fine Arts Camp in Twin Lake, Michigan.

The trip to Europe in 1994 was an incredible experience. I made great friends and my worldview opened to a much broader (and international) perspective. While in Germany and Belgium, we would stay with host families in the towns where we performed our concerts. The families were so welcoming and gracious of our presence. One of our stops was Hamburg, Germany, and another trumpet player and I stayed with a family which had a young adult son. He wanted to show us a good time while in Hamburg, so he took us to the red-light district of town called the *Reeperbahn*, a German name meaning "rope walk."

First we went out to eat and then we walked up and down a street which I will never forget. Both sides of the street were lined with strip joints, bars, sex toy shops, and pornography stores. It was a land of lust and a dream of darkness. I remember going into a McDonald's restroom on the street corner and finding it lit only with black lights. I asked my host friend why the restroom only had black lights, and he said it was to help prevent people from shooting up drugs there.

After walking for a while up the street, our host led us into a pornography store. It was filled with video after video of porn. As we were walking inside the store, we came upon a booth drawn over with a curtain. Here one could go inside, insert some *Deutsche Marks* and enjoy pornographic video. Our host, his two friends, and my fellow trumpeter entered the booth, pulling out their money. They asked me if I wanted to join them. I got out my wallet, opened it up, and then stopped.

I said, "No, I'm good," and put my wallet away. Later we were walking again down the street and I said to one of my host's friends how I felt quite sad about what was going on here. I didn't understand how everyone could walk about with such lustful dispositions without remorse or shame. I said to him that I thought it wasn't right and that it wasn't the way things were meant to be with us human beings.

As we continued on our way, I was approached by a young woman who spoke to me in German. My host informed me that she was prostituting herself and was inviting me to come with her. I declined without a second thought—except one of great sorrow for her and her kin—and we continued on our way.

We came up to this maze-like barrier which emptied into an alleyway. Signs indicated that men only were allowed past this point into the alleyway. We walked through the barrier and entered what was an alley of storefront prostitution. Women were sitting all along both sides of the alley in these large windows, dressed in lingerie and perched in chairs like animals in a zoo. Men would approach the women at their window posts and talk over price and services.

It seemed like a meat market of human flesh and the voice of conscience within me confirmed the depraved character of my surroundings. There was so much more to life than this.

In front of the main stage at Blue Lake Fine Arts Camp following the final performance of our international band tour.

Waffle House

During Christmas break of my sophomore year of high school, our high school band took a trip to Disney World in Orlando, Florida, to play a couple concerts and to enjoy the theme park. We took coach buses through the night in order to get there. Oftentimes, teenagers are amused by the most random things. It was no different with us back in 1993. For the entire trip, we exhibited a fascination with Waffle House restaurants. Every time the bus would pass one on the highway, we would all raise our arms repeatedly and shout, "Waffle House! Haaaaaaay!"

On the trip back home from Disney World, the bus stopped for breakfast somewhere in Kentucky. And guess what one of the restaurant options was at that stop—you got it: Waffle House! Those of us who had developed an obsession with these restaurants were especially delighted.

For some reason I was one of the last to leave the bus to join up with the others who had gone on ahead to get their tables at the Waffle House. As I exited the bus, I stepped onto a lightly snow-covered ground and saw that in order to get to the Waffle House, one had to walk for quite some distance alongside a waist-high barbed wire fence.

So I began to walk along the fence line toward the restaurant. I could smell waffles and fresh maple syrup in the air. As I neared the restaurant on the other side of the fence, I could see all of my companions happily seated at their tables right in front of the large glass window of the restaurant. I waved to them and they waved to me. Then I stopped . . .

I suddenly had an awesome idea! What if I were to get a running start and hurdle this waist-high barbed wire fence?! Yes indeed! Another moment of glory at the tips of my toes! After all, I had run the 300-meter hurdles for the track team. This should be no big deal, and I had an entire restaurant of people watching.

Next I signaled to my *compadres* what I was intending to do. I could see that there were mixed feelings on the other side of the glass. Some of my friends were waving me off, and, reading their lips, they were saying: "No! Don't do it!" Some of my other friends were gesturing that I jump, saying, "Ya! Come on over!" The elderly patrons of the Waffle House looked stunned and seemed incredulous that someone would attempt something so foolish and risky. The entire scene was unfolding in slow motion.

I was up for the challenge. So, I went back a few paces to get a running start up to the fence with the world watching. My start was solid, but, as I took my final step to lunge over the fence, my shoe slipped on the snow-covered grass and I no longer had clearance! Up I went, suspended in mid-air over the fence, only to snag my jeans (and flesh) on the barbed wire (the scar is still there beneath my left buttock)! I was snagged on the fence and hanging there for what seemed like a lifetime. Embarrassed and mortified, I somehow released myself from the fence and ran into the restaurant as fast as my shaking legs would take me.

At least I was a hero for trying, even if a clown hero with the world watching.

The Bomb

Throughout high school, there were days—many days—when I basically thought that I was "the bomb," or to put it another way, "the shiz-nit!" During my junior year I was flying high: starting quarterback of the football team, first trumpet in the band, scoring top-notch grades, class president. Perhaps I was turning into a bona fide Francisco Turner after all!

I would wear this varsity letterman jacket every day which had my band letter on the right side and my athletic letter on the left. Every medal

I earned from solo and ensemble performances, band, and athletic competitions would be sewn onto those letters and then dangle and jingle as I walked with incessant pride through the halls of Lake Michigan Catholic High School.

I felt unstoppable and that momentum was in my favor. It was just a matter of time and I would be shining at the Golden Dome, *like* the Golden Dome, in South Bend, Indiana. Yet I was living in a bubble and I didn't even know it.

Metatarsals

It was the penultimate game of the regular season of my junior year. We were playing the New Buffalo Bisons away. I remember standing on the sideline before the game, looking out over the field to the opposing team's bleachers. There were maybe a couple hundred fans at most, and I wondered if my Notre Dame vision was only a pipe dream after all. In any case, I was ready to take it to the Bisons that night.

The Lakers came out firing with our signature option game. I was gaining yards on quarterback keeps like no one's business that night. We were dominating the Bisons on offense—until a tragic play that would put me out of commission for months to come.

It was an option right, and I ran the ball for over a dozen yards down the field and then was tackled by a New Buffalo defender. He had landed on my lower legs and feet and I felt this tackle more than any other before. My left foot throbbed with excruciating pain and I tried to stand on it but to no avail. I was clearly out of the game.

My Mom drove me to the hospital in Saint Joseph while we listened to the game on the radio. I was pleased to hear that the Lakers were still overpowering the Bisons. The x-ray at the hospital showed that three metatarsals had been severely fractured in my left foot. My foot was then put in traction and later I was visited by the coaching staff with the good news that we had won the game.

I would go through foot surgery, temporary pins, and six casts before I was able to walk again. Yet I knew that I still had my senior year and I would be fully recovered by then.

My brother, Mike, and I to spectate for the final home football game at Dickinson Stadium in 1994, following my debilitating foot injury during the previous game against the New Buffalo Bisons.

Beach Bum

Growing up on the shores of Lake Michigan, I would often go down to the beach to swim, have quiet time, and throw the football. There were these two posts which stuck out of the sand side by side and I would put a Notre Dame football jersey over the posts and throw passes at it—thousands of passes. For some reason, I preferred to throw passes and shoot baskets alone rather than calling up a friend and getting together.

Shooting hoops next door at the Eberly home
against makeshift defenders.

Likewise, I spent hours shooting baskets a few houses down at the home of the Hughes's. Retired judge, Julian Hughes, would often come out into the driveway to smoke his pipe and watch me shoot baskets. Every so often he would say, "That-a-way, Donny!" I felt as though surrounded by cheerleaders my whole life and that their contentment and that of the whole world rested squarely on my shoulders. It was as if the happiness of the world depended on my academic, athletic, and musical success.

I enjoyed being alone with my dreams. I enjoyed imagining what the future might hold and how I could determine in some way what the future would hold. All this time of solitude had a prayerfulness about it. I was alone yet not alone. I believed that God had everything to do with destiny but assumed that my crystal-clear dreams revealed that destiny.

As a young person, I tended to live in the future most of the time rather than in the present. The quality of my present was determined by the promise of my future. If I was indeed to fulfill my dream—and the world's dream (though the world didn't know it)—of playing quarterback at the University of Notre Dame, then I was of value in the present. The thought of failure was unthinkable and life depended on the openness of the future and the truth of possibility.

A sketch of my dream fulfilled that I made sometime
during my early high school years.

Road to Life

In the spring of my junior year of high school, my good friend Creagon Muldoon invited me to his Protestant youth group. Creagon was two years younger than I, and I was grateful that he extended this invitation to me. Growing up in the Catholic Church, I was not familiar with the format of a regularly meeting youth group, or Bible studies, or going to church on Wednesday and Sunday night as well as on Sunday morning. It was all new to me, but I was willing to check it out. The closest thing we did to a youth group event in my home church of Saint John the Evangelist in Benton Harbor was to decorate Fr. Adams's Christmas tree and eat pizza afterwards. I recall only my brother and I and two other boys (who were also brothers) attending this event!

The first Wednesday night, I came with Creagon to his youth group meeting at Road to Life Church in Saint Joseph, Michigan, I wasn't sure what to expect. After walking up a stairway, I entered a small carpeted room with several rows of chairs and a lectern in front of them. There was a high-pitched ceiling with pendants of all of the local high school teams pinned to the ceiling. There were posters hanging all around the room with Bible verses and messages about chastity and waiting to have sex until you were married. There was also a Yield sign in the back of the room that said "Yield to Jesus." I felt unusually at home in this room and that feeling would grow more and more as time went on.

At the front of the room near the lectern were two adult men, one about forty years old and the other in his twenties or early thirties. They were beaming with joy and were so excited that I had come. They learned my name immediately and asked many questions about my life. Then the meeting got started.

The way they prayed seemed so genuine. It was a spontaneous kind of prayer, saying to God whatever came to mind. There were only about eight of us teens there, but the atmosphere was electrifying. After the opening prayer, we sang a couple songs, reading off of an overhead projector and accompanied by a cassette tape recording of the original artists performing their songs. The two songs I remember were "The Basics of Life" by 4Him and "Big House" by Audio Adrenaline.

I had a special bond with the song "Big House" even before coming to Creagon's youth group. I randomly came across it one day watching TV. I was flipping through the channels and must have heard the word "football" and stopped to watch this Christian music video of the song "Big House." I liked the song and even went out and bought the album later on. So, when we sang that song at the youth group, I was pumped! "Big House" is all about the beatific vision of heaven in which everyone belongs, everyone is at peace, everyone has a place and purpose. It proclaims the infinite hospitality of God the Father in relation to his beloved children. It is a clever and compelling proclamation of the Kingdom of God and the fullness of its consummation. It indicates a movement from lonely solitude to blissful communion.

This song spoke a lot to me about the goodness of God and loving relationships. In many ways it was to me an authentic snapshot of heaven. Lowell and Brian were the tag team youth ministers of this group and there was never a time when they were not excited to be there. They were eccentric about expressing the joy they had in their faith, and, for some reason, I liked it.

One night at youth group, Lowell stood up on a chair in the middle of his mini-sermon to make his point more emphatically. That gesture stuck with me, and I knew he was totally serious and committed to what he believed. On another occasion, I remember being invited to come up front and share a bit about myself with the group of eight or so teens. This, too, meant a lot to me, because I got the sense that the people there cared about me personally and wanted to know me better. In addition to these experiences, the church had a carpeted basketball court—and I loved to play basketball! This was another thing that kept me coming to youth group just about every week.

Looking back, I am so thankful that Creagon invited me to his youth group. It helped me to grow leaps and bounds in my faith and introduced me to a way of reading and feeding on Scripture which I had never known before.

Around this same time, the woman who cleaned my family's house once every week, named Joyce, encouraged me to read through the Book of Proverbs by reading one chapter in the morning and one chapter at night before I went to bed. She was a woman of deep faith. She was always listening to Christian music as she cleaned in our home. At first, this music seemed to offend me, but, as time went on, I came to choose to listen to it myself. I ended up reading through the entire Book of Proverbs and so many more. Thank you for your witness, Joyce.

Rise Up and Walk

On another night at Creagon's youth group, we watched the 1994 movie, *Rise Up and Walk: The Dennis Byrd Story*. It was the story of a New York Jet football player who was initially paralyzed during a play in a game, but then miraculously and through much rehabilitation recovered to the point of walking again. This impacted me significantly as I witnessed an athlete who was so much into his faith. He even would draw the ichthus symbol with marker on his taped-up ankles for game days. I took after this practice and drew these symbols on my ankle braces for high school basketball games. Even though my faith was latent within me, it occasionally expressed itself in bold and countercultural ways.

Shakespeare's Pizza Hut

Oftentimes after varsity basketball games, the team and some of the student body would go out for pizza at the local Pizza Hut restaurant. On one occasion, I was feeling especially studious—which is how I tended to feel most of the time—and I brought in my copy of Shakespeare's *Othello* book that we were reading for my British literature class.

While innocently reading the text under the table amidst much animated conversation all around me, I was accosted by a teammate who was a year older than me. He pulled the book out of my hands and threw it on the floor! He said, "Wonny, what are you doing?! Reading Shakespeare at Pizza Hut?!" It was embarrassing, to say the least, but sometimes I didn't mind being embarrassed if the occasion sent a message to those watching. I still love that Shakespeare.

Pushups

During the summer between my junior and senior years of high school, I attended a co-ed basketball camp in Angola, Indiana, at Trine University. I remember several things that happened at that camp. The first is that a guest speaker and coach made 199 out of 200 free throws right before our eyes as he talked to us about focus, determination, and hard work. That was truly amazing. I've never seen anything like it since.

Second, our resident coach on our dorm room floor warned us at the beginning of camp that if we misbehaved, we would have to go out in the middle of the night and fetch a basketball that he would dropkick deep into a dark wide-open field. Sure enough, later at camp, I was summoned one night to track down a drop-kicked basketball (though I cannot remember the reason why)!

Third, later in the camp another guest coach was talking to the entire group of campers—boys and girls combined. My team was called upon for the coach's demonstration of a buzzer-beater play in which one team member was selected to sink the three-point basket to win the imagined game. The lot fell to me and this was the pivotal time at which to come out as the hero or the dunce.

We ran the play, the ball was passed to me, up went the shot—and—miss! The deal was that if I missed the shot, I would have to go down on the ground and do ten push-ups in front of everyone. After missing the shot, I went down on the ground to do my push-ups, but I decided to do five instead of ten while the coach kept on talking to the group. I thought I would come across to my peers as cool, and I thought I had gotten away with it.

The entire group of boy campers was dismissed and, as we were walking to our next session across the outdoor basketball courts, the camp counselors had the whole group of boys stop. I was called out in front of everyone—I thought perhaps to try the three-point shot again until I made it? Instead I was ridiculed in front of everyone for disrespecting the guest coach and ordered to go down on the hard cement and do fifty push-ups!

At that very moment the entire throng of girl campers walked by looking at the scene in disbelief and disgust. Talk about eating humble pie! But I deserved it.

Red Sox

During the same summer I spent two weeks at the National Youth Leadership Forum on Medicine, hosted by Simmons College in Boston. It was a wonderful time which helped me to further discern if I truly had a vocation to medicine or not. I met some awesome friends from Minnesota, Kentucky, Alabama, and New Jersey. There were many diverse experiences such as seeing a cadaver and a severed head at Brown Medical School, hearing a woman who had AIDS give her testimony, visiting a Pediatric wing of a hospital and meeting with a group of physicians who worked there, and going to a Boston Red Sox game.

Of course, I brought my football with me and remember playing lots of catch with friends during free time. I even remember being out late at night by myself in a dark alleyway, training with my Strength Shoes and jump rope. I never ceased to train for my dreams.

Indeed, my "sox" were red with fire—burning around anxious feet that couldn't move into the future fast enough.

CHAPTER 3

BUCKET FULL OF DREAMS

Man of Promise

A STADIUM IS THE road to earthly stardom. Throughout human history, a stadium also has been the road to heavenly martyrdom. Sometime during my junior/senior years of high school, my Dad invited my brother, Mike, and I to go with him to a Promise Keepers weekend conference at Soldier Field—home of the Chicago Bears! Being raised a diehard Green Bay Packer fan—our blood ran green and gold—the location of this conference was paradoxical, to say the least.

My Mom and Dad had been growing in their faith and relationship with Christ quite a bit through their Bible Study Fellowship (BSF) and Experiencing God groups that were organized by First Church of God on Niles Road, Saint Joseph, Michigan. Over time, our passion for Christ was something my Dad and I held in common.

The purpose of the Promise Keepers movement was to empower men to be faithful husbands, fathers, and followers of Christ. Founded in 1990 by a former college football coach, Bill McCartney, this movement attracted thousands of men to gather together to worship God, to reform their lives through grace and repentance, to renounce racism, and to bond together in solidarity and accountability in carrying out their renewed mission as men of God.

I remember being in Soldier Field and having mixed feelings of my NFL ambitions and God's vocation for my life. Something continued to shift in me. An opening in my soul dilated, making greater room for someone else other than myself.

My Dad would invite Mike and I to attend a second Promise Keepers conference with him, this time at the Silverdome in Pontiac, Michigan—home of the Detroit Lions. These events inspired in me a deeper faith and showed me that it was possible for men to turn over their lives to Christ with great sincerity, and for there to be racial reconciliation among brothers. It was potent, but it would take time for this new dream to supplant the old one, and for the helmet to give way to the heart.

Duplicitous Donny

It was the summer of '95 and getting closer to the now-or-never of my initiation into Notre Dame glory. I would attend Notre Dame summer football camp for the last time of my life. If they weren't going to recruit me, perhaps I could get the coaching staff's attention by shining at their summer camp. Whether or not I got the attention of any of the ND coaches, I certainly got the attention of my quarterback peers. I recall the reaction of one quarterback competitor during a throwing drill. After throwing perfect spiral after perfect spiral, I returned to the back of the line, only to be greeted by the chagrin of my teenage colleague: "Where the hell are you from?!"

Later on during summer camp, Notre Dame tight end, Oscar McBride, addressed the group of campers. We were sitting in a large room together, collectively bedazzled by the glowing presence of a Notre Dame starting football player. Suddenly my roommate who was sitting next to me barfed that day's food intake onto the floor. Everyone in the room, including Oscar, stared in our direction in surprise. Instead of asking if my roommate was okay and helping him back to our room, I gawked at him like the rest and simply got out of his way so that he could leave the room. I continued to listen to McBride's talk with mixed feelings of admiration, concern, and shame.

I vaguely remember apologizing to my roommate that night for not helping him out more. He said it was no big deal. One last serendipitous thing would happen during that summer camp: my roommate and I ended up on the same 7-on-7 team for the camp tournament—he was a receiver and I, the quarterback. Our team won our way to the championship game—right there on the Notre Dame practice field! Not only did we make it to the final game, but we won the championship for our age group! I clearly remember lofting a perfect pass to my roommate (met with a perfect catch) for a game-clinching touchdown. To this day, I have the corduroy Notre Dame football hat awarded to each of us on the championship team.

Coach Lou Holtz and I at Notre Dame's 1994
summer football camp.

Donny Wallenhana

When senior year came around, I was ready to pounce on my destiny. I began to be recruited by Division I schools to come and play football. I remember the very first recruiting call I received was from Cornell University and the very first recruiting letter I received was from Northwestern University. The problem was that many of the letters addressed to me had my name spelled wrong: Donny Wallenhana! Talk about taking the wind out of your sails (at least some of it).

In any case, our head football coach, Phil Brooks, recommended me on the recruiting lists as a Division I caliber athlete. I couldn't have agreed with him more. My Dad worked so hard at putting together a highlight film of my greatest plays from my high school football career. He sent VHS tapes to schools all across the country. I ended up getting phone calls from West Virginia University, Boston College, Army, Navy, University of Toledo, Western

Michigan University, Harvard University, Cornell University, and the list went on. Football coaches would visit me at my high school, and I would be pulled out of class to talk with them. I even met with an assistant coach from Harvard in the Holiday Inn lobby in Saint Joseph. But I never heard directly from the place I yearned for the most: Notre Dame.

Looking back, I was a good athlete but lacked the dimensions that would merit the drool of college football coaches. I was a six-foot-nothing, 175 pounds (on a good day), and my forty-yard dash time was 4.70 seconds at best. This was technically not quite Division I caliber, but close. I could wish all I wanted, but I could not make myself any taller. Division I quarterbacks were typically six-foot-three, if not even more towering. The odds were certainly against me, but I wasn't ready to admit it.

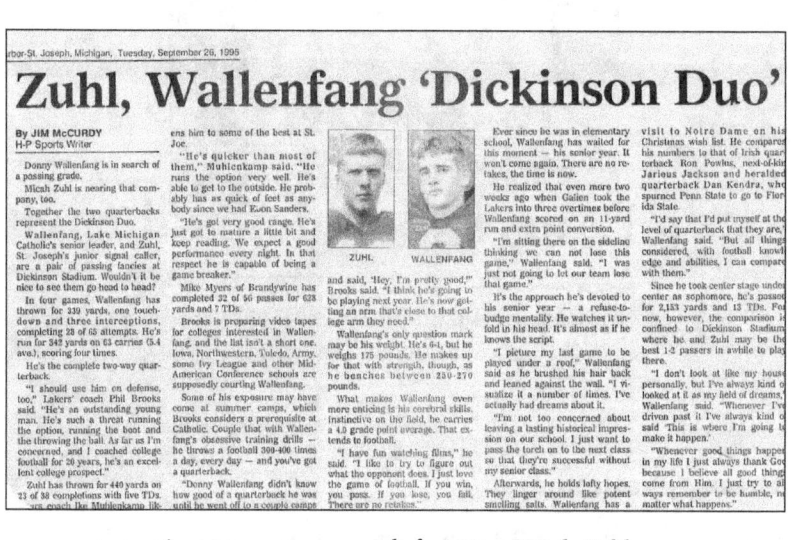

A 1995 newspaper article featuring Micah Zuhl and I as standout local quarterbacks.

Triple Overtime

The most exciting football game which I played in high school was the 1995 contest against the Galien Gaels. The game took place at Galien's home stadium, practically in the middle of a bunch of corn fields. It was the third game of the season of my senior year and our record was 1–1. There was a standing-room-only crowd and the atmosphere was electric. It was a close matchup to the very end, so much so that the game went into three overtimes. Our team played so hard and enjoyed a sweet victory.

That night was a night of celebration and of peace. After having experienced losing season after losing season since junior high, it was so rewarding to come out finally in the winner's bracket. As I recall, I passed for over two-hundred yards and ran for over a hundred yards that game, rushing for multiple touchdowns.

Later on in college, when talking to my friend, Amanda, about the great dilemma of evil in the world created by an all-loving God, I referenced this high school football game as a help to understanding this paradox. I argued that if life always went our way and there was nothing to challenge us—nothing to cause us to dig in deep and persevere and trust—then life would be bland, easy, and lacking in meaning. But if we are faced with countless struggles, suffering, and tests of all sorts, then we are invited to rise beyond ourselves by a power beyond ourselves and make it happen, just like a competition taken into triple overtime.

ON THE RUN: Lake Michigan Catholic quarterback Denny Wallenfang stiff arms Eau Claire tackler Chad Lucas in action Friday night at St. Joseph's Dickinson Stadium. The Lakers defeated the Beavers 20-6.

Turnaround

In seventh grade, I began playing organized football for my school. My initial position was cornerback on the defensive side of the ball. Cornerback is a tough position to play in junior high because many offenses run the sweep in your direction. I was a scrawny kid with high hopes and big dreams. Many times I would get blocked out of the way or miss tackles, resulting in six points for the opposing team.

However, one play seemed to be a turning point in my athletic career. We were playing the Hartford Indians at their place. They were known for having an excellent football program—their high school team won the State Championship in 1993 led by Steve Ackerman, Robert Ledesma, and Dewey Sweat—and 1990 was no exception. The play was coming my way—a sweep right toward the sideline. It was just me and the halfback in the midst of a wide open turf. I had been struggling up to that point in the game and was ready to turn the tide. In front of all of my teammates and coaches on the sidelines, I lowered my shoulder and executed a textbook tackle, bringing the running back down with authority! I distinctly remember Coach Broccolo pumping his fist and shouting, "Good job, Donny! Way to go!"

I recall making a few other tackles during that game and went home proud and content, even though our team lost again.

Our seventh-grade team's record was 1–7. In eighth grade, we went 0–8 with my Dad as the head coach and me as the starting quarterback. In ninth grade, we were 0–9. For my sophomore year, making my debut as the starting varsity quarterback, we went 2–7. My junior year, we went 4–5, and my senior season we pulled out a 6–3 season, just missing the playoffs.

It was definitely a character-building process to go from struggling to win a single game to reaching for the playoffs. My goal was to win a State Championship, just like the Hartford Indians did in 1993, but it was not to be.

WALLENFANG RUMBLES: Lake Michigan Catholic quarterback Don Wallenfang rumbles around end Friday night against New Buffalo at St. Joseph's Dickinson Stadium. Wallenfang rushed for 179 yards and scored one touchdown in leading Lakers to a 24-0 Red Arrow Conference victory.

Midnight Madness

Over Christmas break of my senior year, the high school band once again set sail for Walt Disney World in Orlando, Florida, via coach bus. So, what shenanigan would I pull this time? A real doozy.

It was getting close to lights out in our hotel, and I was playing cards with my friends. One of my friends, Josh, was my go-to receiver on the football team. Even though our senior season was completed, we still had a constant desire to play football.

As we were playing cards, we came up with the idea of sneaking out of the hotel to find a nice big parking lot in which to play catch. The only risk was that if we got caught sneaking out, we would be immediately flown home at our parents' expense! This was a big risk, but we were willing to take it in our adolescent wisdom!

We began to arrange the cards on the table according to the layout of the hotel hallways and then made a plan to make our break. It was successful and we were out the door into the midnight air. Once outside, we ran and hid behind the hotel sign and various parked cars, making our way further from the hotel and safe out of the range of our beloved chaperones.

Sure enough, we found a perfect parking lot with no parked cars and illuminated by giant flood lights. It may well have been Notre Dame Stadium with a full house with the Irish taking on the Florida State Seminoles.

We were in our glory, our hearts aflutter with daring. Now here's where the story gets more interesting . . .

At the far end of the parking lot was a bar. All of a sudden, as we were playing catch, a Ford Mustang peels out from the bar parking lot and races our way! Josh and I take off running back toward the hotel, but we were quite a distance from it at this point. Alongside the road was a Florida forest and we dove into the forest to get out of sight from the road. The Mustang went past, and we slowly emerged from the woods.

About one minute later, another car drives by to pass us and slows down. Again, we make a break for the forest and are feeling quite concerned to say the least. That car drove off and we booked it out of the forest toward the hotel. Suddenly, the same car comes back in the opposite direction and we once again jumped into the woods, by this time laced with cuts from the branches.

As I recall, someone may have gotten out of the car, but I do not remember anyone saying anything. Finally, the car pulled away and we sprinted toward our hotel. As we were hiding behind parked car after parked car, we came upon a parked police car! Luckily no officer was inside, and we were able to make it back to our hotel, through the back door, and into our room.

We certainly regretted our decision to sneak out that night, but it does make for a good story long after the fact!

Notebook

During my senior year, I was taking some tough college prep classes: calculus, physics, advanced literature, and advanced history. For our physics class, we had to turn in our homework notebooks every few weeks. One week, I had two problems which I did not yet finish by the time the day had arrived on which we were to turn in our notebooks.

I was quite concerned about how my points were adding up for the class and the security of my A grade. So, I decided not to turn in my notebook with the rest and to slip it in the pile some other way—namely, through the help of my teacher's son, who was also a senior but not in the class.

The teacher's son, at the behest of my coercion, was willing to go along with my plan and he did successfully slide my notebook in with the rest. In retrospect, I'm so sorry and ashamed that I asked him to do that for me!

A couple days later, when it came time for receiving our notebooks back from our teacher, she asked to talk with me outside of the classroom. She asked if I had turned in my notebook with the rest of the class notebooks because she did not find it among those of my class. I lied and said that I had turned it in with the rest. She seemed to believe me and that was that.

It was indeed sinister what I did as the truth is worth so much more than anything else.

Working away at the desk in my bedroom at the end of my senior year of high school.

Open Heart Surgery

At the end of second grade, I gave my teacher, Mrs. Bentham, a special gift: one coupon for free open-heart surgery! This gift was contingent on me becoming a heart surgeon, of course. But even in second grade, I had no doubt about this contingency and its future fulfillment.

Later on, during my senior year, I was granted the opportunity to observe a live open-heart surgery performed by Dr. O'Dorisio. The surgeon was very gracious in letting me watch this surgery and took time with me beforehand to outline on paper the bypass procedure he would conduct. It was a tremendous experience. Following the surgery, my dream was still alive to be a cardiologist someday.

Bucket Full of Dreams

During my senior year of high school, still clinging to my dream to play quarterback at Notre Dame, I received a call from a close family friend, Jim Muldoon. He said that he wanted to get together over hot chocolate in order to share with me something important. We met one afternoon at Café Tosi in downtown Saint Joseph, and he began to tell me that he had a dream one night which was troubling him.

In his dream, he saw me on a stage in a mad rage. I was screaming and throwing things all around the stage. I was out of control and out of my mind. My anger was bursting through any composure, and I was becoming seriously destructive.

Jim's interpretation of this dream had to do with my insistence of my goal to play football at Notre Dame. He understood that this goal was virtually all I seemed to care about. It was all I thought about, all I talked about, all I worked for night and day. He was concerned about me.

You have to understand that Jim became a sort of conditioning coach for me through high school. It all started with a bet when I was in junior high. Our families were staying at a hotel—I don't remember where or for what reason—and this hotel had a weight room in it. I bet him one night that I could bench press more than he could. If my wager was right, he would have to give me his black cowboy hat. If not, the deal was that he would go with me on my first date!

The next day was the showdown and (of course) he bench pressed more weight than me by a significant margin. However, later on Jim did not end up coming with me on my first date or any date for that matter. To this day he'll never let me forget that I welched on that bet! Over the years, though, Jim would run and go weightlifting with me. He often would say before my athletic contests, "Give 'em hell, Donald!" He really took me under his wing and helped me to become a great athlete.

Back to the dream. Jim understood his dream to be a kind of foretelling of the devastation I would undergo if I did not begin to ease up on my grip of this goal of playing quarterback at Notre Dame. Yet Jim also opened my mind to another possibility.

At this time, Jim was growing a lot in his personal faith. He began talking to me at Café Tosi about the idea of God's will—the real possibility (if not actual reality) that God would have a will for my life. The truth was that I had thought about this idea before. I had been introduced to it in my Catholic upbringing, but it had not been something prominent in my life up to that point.

There was a prayer I learned in Miss Borlick's third grade class. Our class even made one of those extended banners and colored in this prayer. We hung it in the front of our classroom. It went like this: "O my God, tell me what you want me to do and help me to do it." There was something that resonated with me about this prayer even from a young age—yet the prayer frightened me. Over the years, even through high school, I could never honestly pray this prayer. What if God wanted me to be a priest? What if God wanted me to be a missionary? What if God was calling me to do something different than the dreams that I held so dear? Up to that point, I could never move myself to pray this prayer with an open heart to God's will.

During our meeting, Jim went on to say that God's will has to do with pouring out our own wills. He illustrated this idea through the analogy of a bucket. He said that each of us is like a bucket and we're filled with different things. In order to be filled with what God wants to fill us with, we must freely empty ourselves as if tipping out the contents of a bucket. If a bucket is filled with water, it must be emptied of that water before being able to be filled with something else. Jim challenged me to examine myself as a bucket and to ask with what I was filled. Was it according to God's will or according to my own?

I remember leaving that meeting with Jim, walking back to my car, and feeling an unusual sense of peace. At that point I saw myself open—only if slightly—to the possibility of seeking God's will for my life with sincerity. Only time would tell how I would respond to this new challenge.

> Living for God, Jesus Christ, and
> walking in His light (doing His Will) is
> more important than anything I could do
> or imagine on my own.
>
> Set your mind on things above, not on
> earthly things.
>
> - Whatever you do, work at it with all your
>   heart as working for the Lord, not for men.
>
> - Humble yourself.
>
> - Die to self.

Notes that I wrote to myself during my senior year of high school.

The Painful Truth

Throughout high school, I would talk with my Mom and Dad (and anyone else who would listen) nonstop about how I was going to play quarterback at Notre Dame. Oftentimes at meals I would launch into my sound arguments as to why it was virtually certain that I would eventually don the #3 jersey at the most highly prized school in the land. My parents would listen to me and even affirmed the conviction of my coveted dream. They were happy that I worked so hard toward a goal that was beyond reproach.

I recall attending a Notre Dame football game with my Dad one Saturday afternoon. As we walked toward the stadium, my Dad said to me, "So this is where you're going to play someday." It was more of a statement than a question as if my destiny were being sealed by his prophecy. "Yes," I said, "it is."

Later on into my senior year of high school, when time was beginning to run out on my dream, I stopped in the senior hallway in desperation to ask one of my beloved teachers, Sr. Mary Ann Rybarczyk, "Sr. Mary Ann, do you believe that I can play quarterback at Notre Dame?" "Yes," she said, "I believe that you can play quarterback at Notre Dame." Sr. Mary Ann bled navy blue and gold and had her classroom walls plastered with Notre Dame paraphernalia. I was constantly seeking that verbal validation from others that reassured me of my confidence and my future.

One day, however, my Dad said words that devastated me within. We were sitting at the dining room table on a Sunday afternoon, and I was going on and on about how I would walk on the Notre Dame squad and eventually become the starting quarterback there. My Dad said to me flat out, "Donny, you're not going to play football at Notre Dame. You're just not big enough." My heart sunk deep within me. Was my Dad going back on his former prophecy? Was he denying every pass and catch we had shared in the front yard? If my Dad was for me and my dream no longer, who else was? Yet there was something in me that agreed with my Dad—the fulfillment of my deepest desire was becoming more and more unrealistic as time went on.

Getting Desperate

On many occasions during my junior and senior years of high school, I would drive down to Notre Dame by myself to visit campus. In particular, I liked to walk around the football practice fields, imagining my future career as a Notre Dame football star. These trips were like little pilgrimages and they had a prayerfulness about them. They helped to assure me of my destiny—seal it in a way due to my unrelenting devotion to this dream. As Dr. Seuss writes in his children's classic, *McElligot's Pool*: "If such a thing could be, it certainly would be." My dream was the most certain possibility as long as it lived in the future.

One winter day during my senior year of high school, I was determined to drop in on the Recruiting Coordinator of the Notre Dame football team, Coach Bob Chmiel. I had gotten to know coach Chmiel from a distance as I religiously read the *Irish Sports Report* on a daily basis. This publication provided the latest detailed updates on the recruiting news for Notre Dame's football team. On this blizzard-like day, I had no certainty whether Coach Chmiel would be in his office or not. I just took a chance of running in to him in order to introduce myself and give him a copy of my football highlight film.

I got dressed in my blue blazer and tie, donned my varsity jacket on top, and set out in my 1980's navy blue Buick Riviera sedan (the Mercedes had since broken down). Off I went south on Route 31. It turns out that it was closed, and I had to take an alternate route. I ended up travelling south on some back country road which I had never driven, a situation compounded by the fact that I am terrible with directions. But somehow I ended up at Notre Dame through the blustery snow and ice.

Once there, I entered the Joyce Center and proceeded to find Coach Chmiel's office. Sure enough I found it and serendipitously he was in! He was meeting with some larger-than-life lineman, and there I was waiting my turn. This was serious and probably my last chance to make a good first impression with a key member of the Notre Dame coaching staff. After he was finished meeting with the lineman, I presented myself with all the determination I could muster.

There was no point at which he seemed impressed—not even for the fact that I randomly showed up on a blizzard-like day! He was blunt and to the point. I inquired into the status of the quarterback recruits which I knew they were pursuing, such as the double-threat running quarterback from Tupelo, Mississippi, Jarious Jackson. Chmiel said that he "wasn't at liberty to say." He then took my VHS highlight reel and had me fill out a typical recruit info card which felt like a sheet of gold in my hands. And that was that.

I thanked him and left his office with perhaps a little more hope than I had upon entering, yet he gave no signals for any serious promise of making the team someday. If I could come across as a Rudy-wanna-be, I thought that the door of my dream might remain open, even if only a crack.

Wynton

Alongside my dreams of athletic prowess and intellectual brilliance was my dream of musical magnificence. Music was a staple in the Wallenfang family as my Grandma Ellen played piano professionally for churches, big bands, and civil events. Her husband, my Grandpa Lee, was a fine clarinet player and also would play big band gigs. All three of their children, including my Dad, played music. When the Wallenfang family would get together for holidays, everyone would pull out their instrument (or voice) and make music.

My Dad originally had played the trumpet and then switched to baritone in his high school band. My Dad also had played quarterback and was on the basketball team in high school. He was always an inspiration to me, and I wanted to be like him. I wanted him to be proud of me. And proud of me he was.

My father's basketball team during his senior year of high school. He is wearing number 32.

In fifth grade, I ended up choosing the trumpet for my band instrument. I still remember the first day I brought it home from school. By the end of the night, I could play a B-flat major scale and I played it until my lips felt like they were falling off my face! Ever since that day, I was determined to be the best musician in the band. Over the years my abilities ended up soaring, and I excelled in music.

In addition to professional athletes, my father, and Doogie Howser, MD, one of my idols was Wynton Marsalis. He was the most popular trumpeter I knew, and I bought up all of his classical CDs. I would listen to his recordings night and day and would try to emulate his sound. On one occasion, I bought one of his jazz recordings (not realizing that he was better known for his jazz playing). I put it in my CD player in the car and the music made me feel rather nauseated. Up to that point, I had not listened to very much jazz. However, over time I would develop a great liking to jazz music and that same CD has become one of my favorite recordings to this day.

As you can see, there were several people I admired, but I still had trouble being myself.

Performing on the trumpet in Saint Joseph Catholic Church and outside a local home for some Christmas caroling, with my Dad on the baritone.

Journal Entries

On September 9, 1994, I wrote the following entry in my junior class English journal:

> I think Notre Dame is the greatest place on earth. I love the Golden Dome, Touchdown Jesus, the Grotto, the Sacred Heart Cathedral, the Log Chapel and everything else about Notre Dame. Its Football Tradition stands above all else. The Golden Helmets symbolizing the great Golden Dome, the Golden pants and the House that Rockne built. Every time I visit Notre Dame, I feel like I'm in heaven.

In response to this entry, my English teacher, Ms. Griffin, commented, "Wow! I think you will do well there."

Here are a few other telling English journal entries from my junior and senior years of high school:

> November 16, 1994—"Do Dreams Become Realities?"
>
> I sit in the quiet of my room; alone; looking at all of the football posters covering my walls. "Someday," I think to myself; "Someday soon." Time keeps on ticking. Things go by so fast.

Sometimes they go the way you want them to go, and sometimes they don't. You have to take the good with the bad and accept reality. Sometimes things are just out of control; out of your reach. Don't worry about those things. Think about the things you can control and make the most out of them. Talent + Very Hard Work = Success

December 20, 1994—"My Dream"

My dream is to play starting quarterback at the University of Notre Dame, to play starting quarterback for the Green Bay Packers, to be married and have a family, to become a doctor and help as many people as I can. You could describe this as my Utopian future.

January 3, 1995—"My Goals"

My goals are to get straight A's every quarter, do well on my SAT and ACT, grow to be 6'2", 190 lbs., win a state championship in basketball and football, be recruited to play football at Notre Dame, and help a lot of people.

February 28, 1995—"Notre Dame"

Notre Dame is awesome! It is my heaven on earth. If I'm feeling sad or depressed, all I have to do is think about Notre Dame and I'll usually feel better. I love to read about Notre Dame football. I like to visualize myself playing for the Irish. I will make it happen.

March 9, 1995—"Me = ND"

I love Notre Dame. My dreams lie at Notre Dame. Tradition is ever present there. God's presence is everywhere. There is a spirit at Notre Dame. It is very evident. You can feel it. It is a spirit of love, joy, companionship and victory. Setting your eyes upon the Golden Dome, the steeple of the Cathedral or Touchdown Jesus gives you a true sense of optimism. Notre Dame is a heaven on earth. Notre Dame has the ability to lift your spirit.

April 5, 1995—"So Many Options"

I thank God for all the many opportunities He has provided in my life. I am very fortunate. I will probably be able to play college football anywhere in the country. If I were to get hurt playing football, I could always play my trumpet anywhere in the country. If I were to permanently cut my lips, I always have my brain which is very valuable.

May 17, 1995—"Accept the Challenge"

What would life be like without tests, homework, challenges or difficulties? It would be a bowl full of cherries, right? I don't think so. Part of me could surely do without those things, but mainly I thrive on them. That is what life is all about—overcoming challenges, succeeding under pressure. You must always have a positive attitude. Find that silver lining in everything. Your dreams will come true.

September 8, 1995—"Dreams Come True"

Dreams do come true. You must work very hard, pray lots and believe in yourself. Thank God for all you have. All good things come from God. When you fail, that's your fault. When you succeed, you can thank God.

September 13, 1995—"Dreams"

Right now I am beginning to actuate my dreams. I am a senior. This is my last year of playing High School football. The first game—but last game was awesome. All of the rest of our games will be awesome too. I am going to make it happen. I have to.

September 27, 1995—"Hartford"

This is it. This is the biggest game of my life so far. We will win it. We have to. I've never beat Hartford in football. My very first game in 7th grade was played against Hartford and they beat us—bad. I'll never forget the 10th grade Hartford game. It's payback time. I'm ready.

October 2, 1995—"Right Now"

Right now, I wish I was in one of those huge bouncy jungle gym things bouncing up and down and all around. I'm very upset and I feel a great emptiness inside. It feels like someone I know died. I know I can't go back but I can go forward. I have no choice. We lost to Hartford.

October 20, 1995—"Excited"

I'm so excited about the game tonight. I want to beat Bangor so bad. We will. I'm going to run all over them and maybe pass a little too. It's raining. That will psyche our defense up. I love football. This is it.

October 23, 1995—"Oh, Man"

Well, we lost to Bangor. Why? What can I do now? My team doesn't seem so upset today but I'm sure there's a part of them that feels sadness. It's hard to accept the fact that one of my major dreams will not come true. That dream is over—history. I'm devastated. This is the worst loss I've ever experienced. It seems like my entire life has been based on this dream and now I know it won't come true. It seems like it's the end of the world as I knew it. All my happiness was based on this dream that is dead and another that is still alive as long as I believe in myself and continue to work very hard.

October 30, 1995—"Halloween"

Wow! This might be the last Halloween I spend at home. Probably not, but I know next year I'll be in college. That's amazing. Football is over, for High School anyway. Well, that's the way it goes.

October 31, 1995—"ND Application"

My Notre Dame application was pretty easy until I got to the essays. The topics are so hard to write about. I'm sick of writing about myself! I have to do a great job on these essays so I can get accepted to Notre Dame.

November 1, 1995—"So Good"

I feel so good because I got my ND application done and mailed. I think I did a really good job on it. I've done all I can to make my dream come true. All I can do now is wait and see what happens. I'm really excited about basketball. I can dunk.

The Office of Undergraduate Admissions sent the following correspondence upon receiving my application:

> **University of Notre Dame**
> Notre Dame, Indiana 46556-5602
>
> Office of Undergraduate Admissions
> Telephone 219-631-7505
>
> November 9, 1995
>
> Donald L. Wallenfang
> 152 Higman Park
> Benton Harbor, MI 49022
>
> Dear Donald,
>
> We are pleased to report that your application for admission is complete and ready for review.
>
> The Committee on Admissions will carefully read your application materials and send a decision to you by Christmas. Please notify us if you have not received a decision letter by December 20, 1995.
>
> We appreciate your interest in Notre Dame!
>
> Sincerely,
>
> Office of Undergraduate Admissions
>
> P.S. If you wish to apply for 1996/97 financial aid from the University of Notre Dame, you must complete two separate forms: the Financial Aid PROFILE and the Free Application for Federal Student Aid (FAFSA). Each must be received by the designated agency by February 15, 1996. If you have questions about financial aid, phone (219) 631-6436.

"So far, so good," I thought to myself. Now we'll just have to wait.

Here are more of my senior English class journal entries during those waiting months:

> November 11, 1995 — "Being a Senior"
>
> As each day passes, I think more and more about where I am in life. I'm finished playing High School football. No playoffs, no State Championship. It's over. What happened? Where did it all go? It was here and now it's gone. I can't believe it. 6–3. ND. There's so much going through my mind. It's all good.
>
> November 21, 1995 — "Right Now"
>
> WIN — What's Important Now
>
> Why is this game important? — It's the game we're playing right now. Right now I should be looking forward to playing in the State Championship High School football game and not the basketball scrimmage against Lakeshore. Battle Creek. Hartford. Bangor. 6–3. It's gone, hopefully not forever. I so much

wish I was still playing football. If I could only go back in time. The long bus rides home. The unfulfilled dreams. The uncompleted job. Why? The intangible goals. Unbelievable. It's now out of my control.

"This too shall pass." → but it might take a while. Think of all the great things you did: New Buffalo, Galien, even Hartford and Bangor. You did a great job. You worked very, very hard. You are a true football player, the epitome of a great football player. Thank God for that. Dad made 40 tapes. Make the most of that. Something good will happen. You've worked so hard. God has a plan for me. Stick with it. Keep a positive attitude. You did great things. Where's Aladdin when you need him?

December 1, 1995—"Banquet"

Last night we had our football banquet. It was awesome. I began to realize what's important. It is important to focus on the great things you did and the experiences you had rather than wondering what could have been. You just have to say, "Oh well, that's the way it goes," and move on.

December 7, 1995—"Recruiting"

Whatever. That's what I have to say about recruiting. I don't like the position I'm in but I have faith that everything will work out just fine. It's all good. If some place doesn't offer me a scholarship, it is because I wouldn't be happy there. I have no control anymore. All I've worked for won't just disappear or amount to nothing.

Notre Dame delivered as promised. I heard back from them before Christmas. Upon receiving the letter from South Bend in the mail, I carried it into my solitude to the top of Piggy Back hill, right near my house. It was a prayerful pilgrimage to the summit of this magical place where we played so many games through childhood. I made the ascent to confront my destiny on the 8 ½ x 11 piece of paper inside the envelope.

I sat on a stump, looking out on a golden sunset over Lake Michigan. I prayed that God would console me no matter what the outcome told by this letter. Here is what it said:

> **University of Notre Dame**
> Notre Dame, Indiana 46556-5602
>
> Office of Undergraduate Admissions
> Telephone 219-631-7505
>
> December 13, 1995
>
> Donald L. Wallenfang
> 152 Higman Park
> Benton Harbor, MI 49022
>
> Dear Donald,
>
> After a careful evaluation of your Early Action application for admission to Notre Dame, the Committee on Admissions has deferred a decision until we can compare your academic and personal attributes with those of our Regular Action applicants. This means that your application will be reviewed again in March. At the end of that month, I will write to you with the Committee's decision. Admission, denial of admission, and placement on the waiting list are the three possible outcomes. I apologize for this delay, but it is unavoidable if we are to give your application the full consideration it deserves.
>
> Between now and the beginning of March, you should send additional information, such as mid-year grades and reports of your most recent achievements. You must pursue admission to other universities because I cannot predict the outcome of our committee meetings. To further complicate the situation, we now anticipate that this year's applicant pool will be among the largest and most talented in our history.
>
> As an Early Action applicant you demonstrated a sincere interest in Notre Dame. All of us here appreciate your sincerity. We hope that you will be patient with us while we continue the formidable task of selecting Notre Dame's freshman class.
>
> Sincerely,
>
> Kevin M. Rooney
> Director of Admissions
>
> mw

I was okay with this. The door wasn't totally closed yet. As I had learned from the Heinz Ketchup commercial, "Good things come to those who wait." But who likes to wait?! More anxious—yet very hopeful—waiting would follow—months of waiting, hoping, and praying.

I had many conversations with my Mom, usually after eating dinner at the dining room table. She and I would linger and talk about our hopes for the future—actually, we probably talked more about my dreams than anything else as we watched the sun sink into the waters of Lake Michigan out our large dining room window.

One day, I remember feeling especially upset and losing hope. I was sitting at the desk of my bedroom—a bedroom caked with football posters and pictures of Notre Dame. I was crying, facing the Bible, and wondering where God was as I began to feel my dreams slipping through my fingertips.

My Mom came into my room and sat on the bed. In my rage of emotion, I shouted to her, "Where is he, Mom?! Where is he?!" I was referring to God. She said, "I don't know."

Livin' on a Prayer

The following are additional senior English class journal entries during this time of patient waiting:

January 2, 1996—"96"

Well, here we are. 1996. Unbelievable. It came so fast, so unexpected. I woke up in the morning and a shiver went through me as I looked at the picture of Kevin McDougal running towards daylight against Michigan. There is no closer feeling of heaven on earth. This year is the beginning of a great experience.

January 3, 1996—"Walk the Walk"

I walk along the beach. It is warm. The sun shines brilliantly in the open blue sky. The waves roll into the shore. I feel at ease. All of my burdens have been relieved. My dreams are still before me. I must meet the challenge. Look straight ahead and push everything else aside. Focus on your mission. I can fly.

January 23, 1996—"A Prayer"

Dear God, please help me to understand. Help me to realize what your plan is for me. I know that you work in mysterious ways. I see a clear path to my dreams, but maybe you would like me to travel the scenic route so I can learn and grow in my faith. Whatever happens, Dear Lord, please be with me and help me to live your Will for me. <>< Amen.

January 24, 1996—"David and Goliath"

I am not getting offers from Division I-A schools because they feel I am not tall enough. I am about 6'0" tall in my stocking feet and these big-time colleges like their quarterbacks to be 6'3" and taller. I truly believe that God has made me this tall for a reason. But just as David defeated Goliath, I will defeat my odds and obstacles.

February 5, 1996—"Good"

These things are good to me: God, my family, school, teachers, wisdom, football, children, values, belonging, challenge, dunking, happy, books (good books), the Bible, Youth Group, God's creations and friends (loyal friends). Humility.

February 6, 1996—"Bad"

Bad things: greed, lust, jealousy, hate, anger, fear, judging others, hypocrisy, atheism, guilt, confusion, depression, freezing, sin and laziness.

February 14, 1996—"Why?"

What do you do when you realize reality? That's what I'd like to know. I don't like the way things are now. I don't like how my life is going. It isn't flowing. What happened to '95? What happened to Nitro 16? What's so amazing about this Senior year? ". . . and these three remain: faith, hope and love. And the greatest of these is love."

February 15, 1996—"Yes"

Notre Dame ended up scholarshipping only one QB this year. His name is Eric Chappell. He's from Montgomery, Alabama. He's 6'5", 220. But, he'll probably end up playing TE or OL. I also found out that Jarious Jackson will be playing some WR next year. All I can say is that the Lord works in mysterious ways.

February 16, 1996—"Friendship"

Friendship is a great thing. Life would be meaningless without friends. A friend is someone who is willing to sacrifice in order to satisfy the other friend's wants. Coercion does not exist within the boundaries of friendship. Friendship is not a relationship based on reciprocation, but rather on love.

February 21, 1996—"Oblivion"

My future is oblivion. I must start setting some new goals soon. Growing up through High School, my future seemed to be set in stone: Championships, Notre Dame, Greatness, Perfection. Those are excellent aspirations, which I believe were created in me by God. I may not achieve exactly what I want, but after all, my life is in the Lord's hands.

March 6, 1996—"WHATEVER"

Ok. Sure. Whatever. Anyways. It's all good. That's what I say when I get in one of those situations where I really don't know what to say. It is a statement of thoughtlessness. It recognizes fate.

In the Meantime

While waiting to hear back from Notre Dame, I knew I had to put my eggs in other baskets besides that one. Even though I was being recruited to play football at several schools across the country, I set my sights on local schools in the Midwest. My final list of schools other than Notre Dame included Elmhurst College, Hillsdale College, Grand Valley State University, Ferris State University, Hope College, and Albion College. I visited all of these schools and more on recruiting trips. It was my final college visit which proved the most meaningful: Albion College.

Located in south central Michigan, Albion College was one of the last places I thought would garner my interest. However, the head football coach there, Pete Schmidt, was a man of integrity and class. He impressed me and took a sincere interest in me as a student athlete. When I met with him in his office, he told me that he was good friends with Washington Redskins head coach, Norv Turner. He also said that he recently had dinner with Coach Turner and Jim Harbaugh, the starting quarterback of the Indianapolis Colts. He assured me that one could make it to the NFL even through a small Division III school. Many players had done this, so it wasn't an entirely unprecedented phenomenon.

My visit to Albion College was awesome. Not only did I have encouraging meetings with the coaching staff, I was very impressed with the professors, the admissions staff, and the students who hosted me. I stayed with Sam Talsma, who was from River Valley High School in southwest Michigan. He and his buddies were such great hosts—so genuine and sincere. We hung out that night in the student union and I had a real sense of the warm college experience that one would hope for. When it came time for me to leave, I realized that I felt at home there. It was strange, but a feeling of assurance overcame me.

My Dad and brother, Mike, came to pick me up in the minivan. One of the first things they said to me was that I received a letter from Notre Dame. It was almost anticlimactic. I was more interested in talking to them about the great time I had at Albion than reading the letter from Notre

Dame. I opened it up nonchalantly in the van on the way to McDonald's, and this is what it read:

University of Notre Dame
Notre Dame, Indiana 46556-5602

Office of Undergraduate Admissions
Telephone 219-631-7505

March 29, 1996

Donald L. Wallenfang
152 Higman Park
Benton Harbor, MI 49022

Dear Donald,

Personal experience has taught me how disappointing it is to apply for something important and receive an unfavorable reply. Thus, I am sorry to report that the Committee on Admissions has not approved your application for admission to Notre Dame.

This year, thousands of eager and talented students are seeking admission to the University. As a result of having an exceptional pool of applicants competing for a limited number of openings, we are forced to select only some from among the many who would be able to succeed here. To accomplish this challenging task, we read every application several times so that we can give each applicant the most careful consideration possible before reaching a final decision. While making these difficult decisions, we often regret that we must deny admission to so many good candidates, especially when we realize how frequently our loss will prove to be another university's gain.

Although our decision on your application is probably discouraging to you at this moment, I am confident that you will overcome this temporary setback and achieve great success during your college years. I appreciate your sincere interest in Notre Dame and wish you well in all your endeavors.

Sincerely,

Kevin M. Rooney
Director of Admissions

mw

The funny thing was that it didn't strike me as devastating in the least! Somehow, I had been prepared for this news and it was my visit to Albion which turned the tide of my most coveted dream. I was fine—not angry, not depressed, not suicidal. I shared the letter with my Dad and brother at Mickie D's and they expected me to have a breakdown. They looked at me stunned, and shared words of reassurance which I didn't even seem to need at that point. We ate our meal, headed home, and that was that.

CHAPTER 4 ─────────────

CROSSROADS

Newspaper

WHAT IS IT ABOUT the newspaper phenomenon—getting your name and your picture in the paper? Why is it such a coveted occasion? Throughout high school, this phenomenon sustained me week in and week out. Seeing my name appear in the sports section—an article, a blurb—I felt like I was noticed, like I was someone, maybe even someone important.

No doubt, newspaper appearances fed my ego and kept my hopes alive for bigger and better things ahead.

After a basketball game, our Lakers team was riding back to school on the bus and one of my teammates had a copy of the *Detroit Free Press*. I said to him, "I bet my name's in that paper." Everyone was like, "yeah, right," and we scanned the sports section, and, sure enough, there is was in fine print: "Donny Wallenfang, QB, All-State Honorable Mention." At least I was mentioned...

LOOSE BALL: Lake Michigan Catholic's Donny Wallenfang (52) attempts to gain control of the ball as Michigan Lutheran's Steve Mihalk (42) applies pressure in game Tuesday night. Even though Mihalk scored 29 points, Lutheran came up short as Catholic won the contest 81-68 and upped its record to 8-3.

Resolution

Here are a few of my final senior English class journal entries. They show the peace, lament, and hope I had after my biggest dream had passed without awakening to its reality. One may have thought that I would have died upon the spot when finding out that Notre Dame wasn't going to happen. Instead what began was a calm trust in God's will and that God's will was better than anything I could ask or imagine.

> April 16, 1996—"OK"
>
> Finally, I'm back in my journal. I've missed it, I guess. Mexico was awesome and things are going pretty well now. I know where I'm going to college—Albion College. I really like it there. It's the perfect fit for me. I'm thankful to be going there.
>
> May 3, 1996—"Original"
>
>> Yesterday, all my troubles—they seemed so far away.
>> But now, it seems as though they're here to stay.
>> How I believe in yesterday.

> Suddenly, I'm not half the man I used to be.
> There's a shadow hanging over me.
> Oh yesterday came suddenly.
> And I know I can't go back, because yesterday is gone
> but tomorrow is on the way.

May 9, 1996—"My Father's House"

> It's a Big, Big House
> With lots and lots of room
> A Big, Big table
> With lots and lots of food
> A Big, Big yard
> Where we can play football
> A Big, Big house
> It's my Father's House

It is remarkable to read my final journal entry which quotes the lyrics of the Audio Adrenaline song, "Big House." It really sums up the shift of my dream. I was beginning to wake up to a reality that was even better than my greatest wish up until that point: the Kingdom of God.

Breakfast of Champions

The week leading up to high school graduation was full of events to send off the class of '96. One of these events was the senior breakfast at which we received letters that we wrote to ourselves at the end of our freshman year of high school. I had forgotten about these letters, but when they were passed out to us to open and read, I was less than excited to read mine because I could easily recount what I wrote. It all centered on playing football at Notre Dame and that was not happening. Here is the letter I had written to myself three years prior:

> June 1, 1993
>
> Dear Donny,
>
> Hopefully things are going very well. This freshman year was great. Football season was a blast. Basketball wasn't the greatest, but I've learned a lot about mental focus since then. Track was a lot of fun. I did the hurdles for the most part and did pretty well. School is so much fun. I averaged about a 3.87 which is

pretty good. Right now as you sit there and look back into the past years, you probably are smiling and laughing. You're smiling and laughing at all the good times and also all of the stupid mistakes you've made. Well, that's the way it goes, I guess.

If all things went as planned, you're preparing for your freshman year at the University of Notre Dame. You will follow many of the excellent quarterbacks, such as Joe Montana, Joe Theisman, Rick Mirer and Ron Powlus. You have spent a good chunk of your life in the weight room, running the streets at home and in the front yard playing catch with Dad. Hopefully it all paid off. And, if you aren't on your way on this path, God must have something else in mind for you. This is your dream: I want to be the starting quarterback for Notre Dame. This is your goal: I try my best. No matter how the dice turns up, I will never give up. I am the only one who thinks I can make it. No one thinks I can do it but me. It's a lonely road but I just have to believe in myself. Remember what Fran said: "You will be the quarterback for Notre Dame. It's all in your mind, Donny. It's all in your mind." Hard work is what got you here. It's going to take a lot more work to get you even farther.

Don't forget to thank all the people who got you here: God, family, teachers, friends and yourself. Remember all the people who gave you guidance and taught you about life.

I know you can do it. Keep on working, believe in yourself, and you'll get there.

Donny Wallenfang, #3

Even though I had been doing alright with the fact that I wouldn't be going to Notre Dame, this was tough for me to read. I was still so egocentric at this point in my life. I can't remember any of my classmates' reactions to their letters, and I don't remember caring about them. All I remember was my sour reaction to my own letter and wanting the world to feel sorry for me along with me. I was haunted with the accusation of "failure." Was I really a failure? Was I wrong about trusting in God's goodness and God's plan for my life? It would take some time for me to answer these questions with certainty.

Wheelbarrow

Another highlight of graduation week was our Baccalaureate event in Saint Joseph Catholic Church. This is the church in which we would have our school Masses and it was a very significant place to me. During the Baccalaureate rehearsal, Mrs. DaDan said that some of us would need a wheelbarrow to wheel out all of the awards we would receive at Baccalaureate night.

That night came and even my Grandpa Lee and Grandma Ellen were in attendance. My Grandma and I were to play "Ain't Misbehavin'" as part of the program—her on the piano and me on the trumpet. It was a very meaningful and culminating event. One unusual thing happened during our performance. As we were playing, the tassel of my graduation cap got stuck in the corner of my mouth! It stayed there for just about the entire song, but we made it through sounding good all the same!

Throughout the course of the night, I was awarded the John Philip Sousa Band Award (for the best high school musician), the Best Male Athlete Award, the Jennifer Monte Memorial Scholarship (for outstanding academic and service achievement), and one of the Christian witness awards (which was a lapel pin of a colorful rooster, symbolic of announcing Christ in one's daily life). It turns out that I was one of those students who Mrs. DaDan had been referring to. Granted, there were only about sixty students in my graduating class, but I was beaming with pride that night.

Later on, after we had returned home, my Grandma noticed the word "Catholic" on the back of my varsity jacket. It read:

Catholic

Football

Basketball

Track

She asked why I chose to have the word "Catholic" sewn at the top of the jacket. Other than the fact that Francisco Turner had this inscribed at the top of his varsity jacket, I told her that I was proud to be Catholic and that it was the essence of my school's identity and my own. She complimented me for my faith and for my courage to share it, even though deep down I knew that me having faith and courage was a half-truth.

Performing "Ain't Misbehavin'," with my Grandma Ellen Wallenfang accompanying on piano during Baccalaureate night.

Glowing with pride at my graduate reception party.

Jingle Bells

I certainly had a high estimation of myself in high school, especially during my senior year. Perhaps at times I reached out to people, cared enough to ask people how they were doing, maybe even sacrificed for people on occasion. But for the most part, I was as conceited as they come.

I remember walking down the senior hallway every morning, sporting my arsenal of jingling metals on my varsity jacket—one set for athletics and the other for band (the band letter was definitely unusual on a varsity jacket). I was proud of my accomplishments and wanted the world to know all about them. It was a quintessential instance of shameless self-promotion, yet I seemed to be missing something all along.

Io Triumphe

Albion College ended up offering me a Presidential Scholarship and I gladly accepted and made my home there as a Briton. Pre-season football training was intense, and I quickly realized that I was a big fish in a bigger pond than Lake Michigan Catholic High School.

Nevertheless, I was happy there. While at freshman orientation, I was assigned to the "Stars" group (this will have great significance later). I met my roommate-to-be, Ryan Strother, and we hit things off in no time. He would become a great friend and confidant.

Wearing the number 19 as an Albion Briton
while a freshman in college.

iGod

The title of this book, *iGod*, refers to the selfish and myopic life I tended to live before the massive conversion I would undergo during my first year at Albion College. *iGod*—an obvious play on names like iPod, iPad, iPass, etc.—encapsulates the common human symptom of the pandemic of self-centeredness and the temptation to act as our own Lord of the universe. "It's all about me!" Is it really?

This book is ultimately about turning the self inside-out in love and responsibility for the other. In 2013, at thirty-four years of age, I felt moved to begin the writing of this book so that it might be something that would resonate with many people around the world. My hope is that it would be a story that inspires people to reflect on their lives and to find out if they were living as an iGod in a universe which they did not create.

The rest of my story from here on out will become more explicit in its language of faith. The truth is that my conversion has less to do with me than it has to do with the One who made me and has set my heart free. There is indeed a God, and I am not this God. I am moved to tell my tale—at least several meaningful pieces of it—so that you may find some meaning here that relates to your own life and causes you to reflect on it and perhaps even to change.

The next fragment of my life I will share signifies a great turning point, and it's a story I like to tell again and again as it sums up the meaning of conversion—of having a change of heart—and offering the whole of one's life to the God from whom all good things come.

Crossroads

It was a cool and crisp late fall night on the campus of Albion College. I was in my glory as the semester was winding to a close and I was enjoying every minute of college life. That evening I had a meeting scheduled with the head football coach, Pete Schmidt. I had performed fairly well for my first year of college football, and, at the end of our meeting, Coach Schmidt gave me a brand new Wilson 1001 football to work out with during the off-season.

I left that meeting filled with hope for the future and gratitude for the many opportunities to do what I loved in college. Walking back solo to my dorm room in Wesley Hall, I decided to make a stop at Goodrich Chapel. Albion College was loosely affiliated with the Methodist tradition since its founding in 1835, and Goodrich Chapel was a nice place to pray.

The Music Department also was housed in the chapel, so I spent a lot of time there on a daily basis.

One unique place within Goodrich Chapel was the side chapel. It was a mini chapel set off from the main chapel. It had a seventies brown shag carpet, wooden paneling on the walls, a plug-in bubbling fountain, and a large silver cross affixed to the wall in front. I would go there often to pray, read Scripture, and even have Bible studies with friends there. I was a part of InterVarsity Christian Fellowship, Fellowship of Christian Athletes, United Voices of Albion College (a Black Gospel choir), and participated in many other faith events on campus and off.

Pictured beneath the silver cross in the side chapel of Goodrich Chapel with friends gathered for Bible study on the campus of Albion College.

Entering the side chapel on the cool fall night, I had many significant objects on my person. First, there was my backpack full of books. I was a pre-med major at the time and worked very hard (as usual) in my studies. The backpack full of books symbolized my dream of becoming a medical doctor and my love for learning. Second, I had on a Saint Mary's College (South Bend, Indiana) hat which my girlfriend at the time, Anne, gave to me. Anne was attending Saint Mary's College and gave me this gift by which to remember her. She had hand-woven various colors of yarn in the back of the hat and it symbolized our relationship which had begun in the spring of my senior year of high school. Third, I was toting my trumpet that evening as well. It had stickers from Europe on its case from when I went on the international band tour with Blue Lake Fine Arts Camp in 1993. And fourth, I had the new football just given to me by Coach Schmidt.

One by one, I set these objects down at the foot of the cross. I was so thankful and wanted to offer them all to God as a sign of my gratitude. Yet there is always risk when laying something down at the foot of the cross. After all, the cross is first a symbol of death. In this moment, as I laid down all that I held dear beneath the silver cross, I remembered the prayer I had learned in third grade: "O my God, tell me what you want me to do, and help me to do it." That night I may have prayed that prayer openly and honestly for the first time—but not the last.

Urbana-Champagne

Approaching the end of my first semester at Albion College, life was good. My grades were solid, I had awesome friends, and I was looking forward to a nice relaxing Christmas break. As it turned out, Anne and I broke up over the phone sometime after I made that sincere prayer in Goodrich Chapel, shrouded in the nighttime of fall. Even though I was growing leaps and bounds in my faith, I was still rather immature and self-centered. While it was me who initiated the break-up, my coldness and indifference wasn't worthy of any affection whatsoever. Something needed to work on my frozen heart from the inside out.

With Christmas break just a couple weeks away, I received a phone call in my dorm room. It was Andy, one of the graduate discipleship leaders from InterVarsity Christian Fellowship on campus. He wanted to invite me to attend a conference called Urbana. It was to take place over Christmas break in Urbana-Champaign at the University of Illinois. Urbana Conference was dedicated to promoting Christian missionary activity throughout the world.

At first, I thanked Andy for the call, but said that I had other plans for break. He told me to pray about it just a little bit more and to ask whether or not God was telling me not to go. It was an interesting twist of interpretation. Usually, one might ask if God desires you to do this or that. In this case, Andy was approaching the question from the point of the double negative: Perhaps God is not telling me not to go, in which case why not go? Soon thereafter I called Andy back to tell him that I would like to go to the conference after all.

Several friends from InterVarsity ended up on the trip, as well as an outsider whom I had not met before: Kristian Petrovich. At first appearing quiet, smug, and aloof, Kristian would end up undergoing a profound conversion through the course of the conference, and so would I.

A book could be written on this week-long experience alone. God had been at work on me my whole life, but this week in December of 1996 would alter my world like nothing before. It was just a matter of giving myself over to Christ totally, and he would do the rest.

Before the conference, participants were to read Acts of the Apostles from the Bible. During the conference, participants met in assigned small groups every day to discuss the text and also attended short seminars throughout the day. For the most part, participants gathered in the basketball arena for worship, prayer, and to listen to speakers such as George Verwer, Elisabeth Elliot, Jorge Atiencia, Robbie Castleman, Henry Koh, Tokunboh Adeyemo, and T. V. Thomas. I was blown away by the entire experience. I was surrounded by people who were so passionate about their relationship with God that they wanted nothing more than to share their love with the whole world.

Three clear memories from the conference stand out to this day. First, on one of the days of the conference I set out by myself to find a place just off campus to eat lunch. I don't remember where I went for lunch, but I do remember returning to campus and walking through this mystical grove of trees that was bathed in a thick fog. Visibility was low, but I entered this grove of trees to pray: "O my God, tell me what you want me to do and help me to do it."

I was moved to read the end of the Gospel of John—a scene of the resurrected Christ asking Peter, "Do you love me?" Jesus asks Peter this question three times, seeming to invite Peter to deny his denial of Jesus three times. After each time Peter affirms his love for Jesus, Jesus gives him a charge: "Feed my lambs," "Tend my sheep," "Feed my sheep." This passage spoke to me with such depth and clarity that I sensed God was calling me to do the same: to care for his sheep.

Second, I recall one of the greatest talks of the conference being that by T. V. Thomas. At the beginning of his talk, his voice went hoarse to the point that he hardly could speak a word. Dan Harrison, Urbana Director, came up to the podium to give T. V. a throat lozenge and to pray over him. Soon thereafter, T. V.'s voice became as loud and clear as ever, delivering one of the most inspirational talks I have ever heard. The next day, I attended a seminar at which T. V. was presenting, and there was Kristian in the front row, sitting at his feet with a huge smile on his face.

Third, another wonderful talk during the conference was Robbie Castleman's talk on being a bold witness for Christ. She chided the Christian audience for not reading the Bible in its entirety and instead only reading certain passages here and there. She wondered that if our relationship with Christ is the most important thing in our lives, why not read the entire Bible since it is such a vital source for this relationship? So, she challenged everyone to read not just select passages, but to read the entire Bible. Each of us went home with an Urbana Bible that included a one-year Bible reading plan. As December turned to January, I would take Robbie up on her challenge. I ended up reading the entire Bible during the year of 1997. Just as champagne and good wines warm the body from the inside out, the words of Scripture do the same for the soul.

Late Nights in the KC

Returning to campus following the Urbana Conference, the spiritual renewal was electrifying. All of us who went to Urbana were on fire in our faith and concerned for one another like never before. We all toted our Bibles in our backpacks and would stop to pray spontaneously with one another at the drop of a hat. College life took on a whole new meaning: we were there to be witnesses for Christ.

I loved to listen to my fellow students as they talked about their problems and joys. One of the best places to talk on campus was the Kellogg Center, also called the "KC." On many occasions, I would hang out in the KC with friends and talk late into the night—and sometimes into the early morning—about God, life, and just about anything. Later in life, Kristian would marry, have children, and be ordained a priest of the Serbian Orthodox Church.

I remember one night when Kristian, a couple other people, and I were talking about God, and Kristian sat up on the back of a chair and spoke with such passion and conviction. He was growing in his personal faith by leaps and bounds. Coming from an Eastern Orthodox background, he began to study the life and writings of the mystic, Seraphim Rose. He would fast frequently and study Scripture incessantly.

On another memorable evening, I was talking with a new acquaintance, Amanda, testifying to the truth of the Christian faith. At the time, she was an atheist and was being honest about her past and about her struggles. I said to her, "Amanda, time is on God's side!" I jumped up and pumped my fist in the air in celebration of God's goodness and love. She smiled and laughed and said, "Maybe you're right."

Winning, Inc.

It was the summer of 1997. My summer job was to work as a coach and mentor in a non-profit sports and literacy camp called Winning, Inc. It was founded in 1996 by my former high school football coach and biology teacher, Phil Brooks. We would meet in school gyms in Benton Harbor within housing project communities. Kids of all ages would show up for this free camp at which they would learn basketball and reading skills. It was a work of beauty.

I witnessed joy in the face of poverty, abuse, and abandonment. I witnessed laughter in the aftermath of shame and despair. I witnessed hope welling up from souls who were too majestic to believe the lies that haunted them.

A scene with children and I at the summer Winning camp in Benton Harbor, Michigan.

Coach Bobby Simmons—local police officer, former NFL player, and one of my former high school football coaches—also worked at the camps. He had a tremendous joy about life and always knew how to get a smile out of someone. I admired him greatly and still do to this day.

Part of the daily routine of the camp was to give a short motivational talk to the young people in attendance. At the time, I was quite reluctant to speak in public. In fact, throughout elementary, middle, and high school, I was terrified of it. I tended to be shy and my overwhelming obsession with perfectionism prevented me from undue risk taking.

However, one day I mustered up enough courage to address the students. I said something to this effect:

> Isn't it a great opportunity to come together and to play basketball like we do. This is a wonderful gift from God and we can't forget that. All of this makes us think of something deeper. It makes us think about ourselves and how we face one another as different yet united. You are all black. I'm white. Yet altogether we make up a unified mosaic of humanity. God has created us all different and this is something beautiful. Think of a bag of Skittles. What if you opened it and they were all yellow? That wouldn't be as interesting. But because there are so many different colors, the candy comes alive all the more! We are a colored people and for this we can give thanks to God.

At the end of my short speech one of the kids said, "Amen!" That Amen resonates deep in my being to this day.

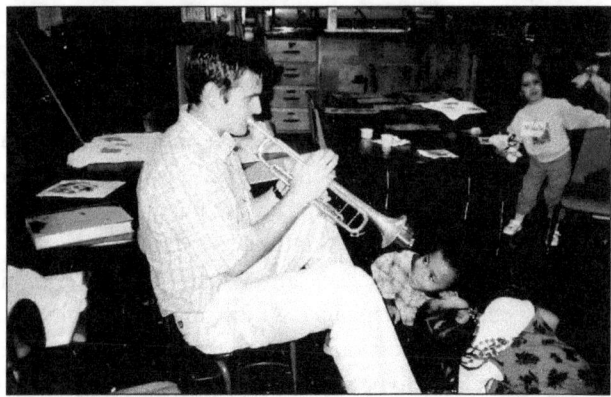

Performing on the trumpet for children at the Readiness Center in Benton Harbor, Michigan.

Bishopric

Over the summer months, I continued to blossom in my Christian faith. I read Scripture constantly and would frequent many church services of many Christian denominations, all the while going to Catholic Mass every Sunday. I still had questions about the Catholic faith that were being raised by my experiences in other non-Catholic Christian denominations. I decided that it was time for me to find out some definite answers, so I thought of no better person to talk with than Bishop Murray of the Diocese of Kalamazoo.

He graciously welcomed me to meet with him. I met him in his office and he fielded my questions one after another. Looking back, I'm sure he had heard these questions many times before: "If we can pray directly to God, why should we pray to saints?"; "Why is Mary so important for the spiritual life?"; "How do you interpret Paul saying, 'not to go beyond what is written' (1 Cor 4:6)?" The bishop patiently answered my questions, and I was thankful for his hospitality in taking the time to meet with me.

I remember departing from the meeting semi-satisfied with his answers. He suggested that I read more from the *Catechism of the Catholic Church*. He said that many of my questions were addressed there, and he even may have given me a copy of the book. He was right, and as I continued to search out answers for these and other questions—indulgences!—I would find answers that made sense and resonated with truth.

Million Man March

On October 4, 1997, a pivotal event happened that was a culmination of the influence of the Promise Keepers movement on my life. On that beautiful fall Saturday, hundreds of thousands of men gathered on the grounds of the National Mall in Washington, DC. I was one of them. My good friend, Kristian Petrovich, and I tagged along with the bus of men sponsored by New Hope Worship Center of Albion, Michigan. Pastor Bill Steere was one of my spiritual mentors at the time, and he, too, went on the prayerful pilgrimage to DC. Kristian and I fasted the entire trip. We road on the coach bus through the night and arrived in DC in the morning.

I remember having a meaningful conversation with Pastor Steere at one of our rest stops. I was sitting down on a curb by myself near the parking area. Pastor Steere walked up to me and sat down on the curb beside me. This meant a lot. That the pastor of this church would take the time—and have the humility!—to sit down on an uncomfortable concrete curb to talk with me meant so much. He wanted to know how I was feeling and what was on my mind.

I told him that I was struggling to make a big decision about the future of my life. At Albion College, I still was majoring in pre-med, growing in my love for music (I had my first music theory class that semester), and playing football for the Britons. Altogether, it was getting to be too much, and I was afraid that I was going to have to let go of one of those three activities that I loved so much and at which I worked so hard.

Pastor Steere, as I remember, seemed to affirm my many gifts and yet, at the same time, admitted that it sounded to him like I was trying to do too much at once. This brief and passing conversation helped relieve me of any sense of guilt or irresponsibility in moving toward giving up one of my three deeply rooted passions in life. Would I give up my pre-med studies, music, or football? Only time would tell.

Wise Fool, Part II

As mentioned above, the term sophomore comes from the Greek words, *sophos* ("wisdom") and *moros* ("dull, sluggish, stupid, foolish"), serving as a fitting term for that second year of high school or college when students are not exactly brand new to things, but neither have they become seasoned veterans. It was my sophomore year at Albion College, and I was hoping to grow more in wisdom and less in foolishness.

Two monumental things happened in my life that year. I ended up changing my major from pre-medicine to music and I met my future wife. Amidst the turbulence of college life, a path was becoming clear as I prayed that God would continue to order my steps.

My college roommate, Ryan, and I.

Cinder Block

I was attracted to medicine and the wonder of the human body at a young age. Ever since I can remember, I gravitated toward what I called "doctor books." In elementary school, I developed a small personal library of medical textbooks. I had the complete set of *The Human Body* by Torstar Books. I had the classic collector's edition of *Gray's Anatomy*. I had a life-size pop-out poster of the human internal anatomy on my bedroom door.

I was intent on becoming a medical doctor throughout my childhood and into college. During my freshman year of college, I fared pretty well. I earned As, excelled in football, and continued to advance in music. Things were looking up.

However, fall semester of sophomore year, 1997, I had organic chemistry, music theory, and football all in the same semester. It wasn't that any of them were too difficult in and of themselves. It was that trying to do all of them at the same time, to the highest degree of performance, was becoming too much. I was spread thin like never before and was feeling more and more pressure to narrow the scope of what I was doing with my time.

This would be a tough decision. How could I let go of any of the three passions of my life? I had to look to a fourth passion that was more important than all the rest: God. I had come to believe that God had a will for my life, and I was desperate to know what it was. It would take much prayer and soul searching to determine the ever-unfolding mystery of God's will.

I clearly remember one bright fall afternoon, after receiving one of my major organic chemistry exams back at the end of class, I took a walk to Victory Park. Never looking at my exam grades right away, I had tucked the exam in my backpack and headed for the top of Victory Hill. It was a pilgrimage of sorts, and I needed clarity.

Football was going pretty well. I had moved positions from quarterback to receiver and was holding my own on the team. Victory Hill was one of our football team's conditioning destinations and a place I would go often to walk and listen to music on my headphones.

Ascending to the top of Victory Hill, I sat down to pray. I asked that God would make it clear to me what direction to go, because I could not continue in several different directions and get anywhere. I had a vision that I was trying to pull a colossal gray cinder block with a rope, and it wasn't budging. I took out my exam to look at the grade: C.

I then understood my pre-medicine coursework to be this futile burden in relation to music and football. The truth was that I was falling in love with music and my music theory class by the day. One thing I began to enjoy more than anything was to play my trumpet or piano or guitar and to pour out my soul through the music. I was fascinated by music theory, how music was so symmetrical, ordered, and even scientific. I loved to study Bach chorales and excelled in ear training, usually scoring perfect on my ear training exams. I was flourishing in music, and it was flourishing in me. I felt called to this field without hesitation. After that day, I would let go of pre-med and declare a music major.

The Blues

Soon after my decisive prayer experience atop Victory Hill, I played a trumpet solo in our jazz band concert which took place, ironically, in the biology lecture hall. It came off great and my spirit was soaring. Following the concert, I walked across campus with one of my organic chemistry professors, Dr. French, who had been in the audience. I told him about my decision to change majors from pre-med to music, and, to my surprise, he was very happy for me. He said right away that he thought I was making the right decision and said that pre-med majors, after all, were "a dime a dozen." He was saying that for my benefit, of course, and it helped me to be even more confident in my change of direction.

One visit to Dr. French's office hours earlier in the semester stands out. I was intrigued about how all life—all mass and energy—was interconnected. I kept asking him questions to try to get to the bottom of the chain of reactions on earth. I was searching for what drove the entire process, what caused it all. My questions led to the conclusion that the sun was the energy source which drove all the rest of life's symbiotic processes. Later, in light of this question, I would come to recognize the truth of the homophone: sun and Son.

James Miley was my professor for music theory, and I have many memories of him looking at us over the upright piano in the front of the classroom through his wire-rimmed glasses as he played some cadence for us to identify. I soon learned the blues scale and my life would never be the same.

Miley said that all of the jazz greats first learn the blues scale, then innumerable other scales and "licks," and then go back to the basic blues scale for their solos. After playing and listening to lots of jazz music, I think he was right.

One of our jazz band concerts at Albion College.

Ladder to Heaven

During football season at Albion College, we had to meet together as a team on Sunday afternoons to go over game films and to go out to the practice fields for some conditioning. It was the dreaded "ladder drill" in which we had to sprint from line to line on the field under a certain amount of time. I remember taking these conditioning exercises quite seriously, as if I would be positioned as a starter by coming in first every time.

Looking back, I probably could have slacked off a bit and crossed the finish line along with the rest of the pack. However, there was something in me that strived for greatness, especially in little things like conditioning drills. I'm not sure how much difference my work ethic made as far as influencing the coach's decisions for playing time.

In any case, I regarded each sprint as an opportunity to witness to Christ. One vivid memory is when I was running full steam toward the finish line with Coach Rundle in view. As sweat saturated my grey practice fatigues, running the final length of the field, I shouted out loud as I ran: "Show them who he is! Show them who he is!"

Her Smile

Fall semester of my sophomore year at Albion College was a time at which I was continuing to meet new friends and grow in my faith all the more. I would attend Saint John's Catholic Church as well as services at Protestant churches where some of my friends attended, including a Black Pentecostal church called John 3:16 Ministries, with Pastor Tim Kurtz.

I had a friend named Kate from back home who went to Albion too. She would attend Mass as well and sometimes we would walk there and back together. One day at lunch in Baldwin Hall, I saw Kate across the cafeteria, sitting with some friends—her suitemates, in fact. I had seen her with these friends before and one of them would always have this huge smile on her face.

This smiley girl seemed so filled with life and joy. She wore a blue fleece jacket and always seemed to have a bounce in her step. So, that day at lunch I boldly walked over to the table of all girls and Kate introduced me to her friends. The smiley girl was named Megan, and I was meeting her finally.

RNA

Soon after, I would see Megan at InterVarsity and other Bible studies on campus. She was from a Protestant background and I could tell that her faith in God was alive. We got to be friends and would often hang out in the cafeteria or in the Kellogg Center when studying. One day at lunch, she was talking about her difficulty in understanding DNA replication in biology class.

As a former pre-med major, I had come to understand this material fairly well and I told Megan that I would be happy to help her understand it too. We would meet from time to time to talk over the material, and I think that she got a better understanding of it, little by little, but it seemed that there was something even more important at stake than understanding genetic code replication.

What that something was, time only could tell . . .

My Life Is in Your Hands

Sophomore year at Albion would include a new twist in my musical and religious experience. I recall sitting in a room with about four other people freshman year to discuss the state of the gospel choir at Albion. It was a remnant of people who were hoping to sustain a gospel choir ministry on campus and abroad. I felt rather out of place at the meeting as I had no previous experience of Black gospel music, but for some reason I was invited to the meeting and for some reason I showed up.

Somehow the gospel choir came together during my sophomore year with bass, drums, piano, over a dozen voices, and even a trumpet! It was student-lead and we called ourselves UVAC—United Voices of Albion College. We participated in a variety of Gospel Extravaganza events and would sing the music of Kirk Franklin and many other gospel composers.

One song that stands out was Franklin's "My Life Is in Your Hands." In this song, he speaks of the radical trust in Jesus through all of life's trials and pains: "no matter what may come my way, my life is in your hands."

The Way to Heaven

A football field is a symbol of life. There are boundaries. There is an end zone, a goal line, a goal post. There is midfield and everything in between. Teams strive to get first downs and to work the ball toward the goal line. To succeed takes much effort and teamwork.

It's been said, "You will perform like you practice." I have found this to be true in all aspects of life. Behind high levels of performance are high levels of practice. If you want to end up a champion, you have to practice like a champion.

One hot day, in the middle of football practice at Albion College, I looked over at the drill with the defensive linemen and linebackers. It was a great display of intensity: bodies locked into one another, helmets crashing together, cleats digging deep into the turf, much grunting and striving and sweating. There was Coach Parker, blowing his whistle and shouting like a charioteer at the athletes. Then he shouted out something I'll never forget: "Everybody wants to go to heaven, but nobody wants to die!"

Isn't this so true? All people desire true paradise, but the only way to inherit it is to sacrifice, to give up one's self—to give up one's body, to die. In order to become a canonized saint, one must die to be up for consideration. Everybody wants to go to heaven, but nobody wants to die.

What's the Good Word?

Locker-room talk. Something less than virtuous? In many cases, yes. However, the locker room can be, on occasion, a place for edification. In my football locker at Albion College, in addition to all of my sweat-soaked fatigues, I kept a special book which I would read from a little before and after practice: *The Bible Promise Book*. I had become acquainted with the tome in high school and would read it often as it offered bite-sized passages from the Bible beneath various topical headings. From it I drew strength, encouragement, and hope as I faced life's daily challenges, including football practice.

Pretty soon some of my teammates took notice of my habit of daily digests from this book and they would ask, "Donny, what's the good word for today?" I wouldn't hesitate to share a passage or two with them. It was a life-giving habit that reminded us of a bigger picture than only our upcoming rival on the football field.

However, with such a public witness to personal faith came opposition and even persecution. On one occasion, the Albion College Britons were on the road for an away game, staying in a hotel overnight as usual. I was sharing a room with a few other teammates and was laying on one of the beds, reading quietly from the Bible. The other guys in the room were channel surfing, on the lookout for something eye-catching. Sure enough they found it and started saying, "Ooooo!"

I figured what they might have encountered, and I did not give one glance toward the television screen. The next thing I knew, the guys were saying playfully, "Donny, have a look at this!" I refused with a smile, but they weren't satisfied with my response. Instead, a couple of the guys picked me up off the bed and carried me in front of the TV. I kept my eyes shut, and they even tried to pry open my eyelids to view the pixel portrayal on the screen.

They were not successful that evening in trying to force me to see something I rather would not see. After their laugh was had, they let me go to return to reading the Bible. I couldn't help but laugh too.

Later on in the season, one of the football coaches—not Coach Parker!—pulled me aside and asked me not to be so open about my faith with my teammates. He said that the linemen weren't smart enough to handle all of this talk about God. He asked me to keep it to myself and to let them just worry about football and blocking people.

In spite of his attempted intervention, I witnessed to Christ and his gospel all the more.

All That Gas

Megan and I would get together often to hang out, sometimes just the two of us, sometimes with mutual friends. She loved to order vanilla ice cream from the Eat Shop with "two sides of Snickers," and I loved to be with her. Our friendship was growing and maturing. First, however, I had to work out some lingering immaturity in myself. As much as I wanted to love more, sometimes my intentions went out valiantly, only to return like a boomerang to "me, myself, and I." Two scenes serve to illustrate these growing pains.

First, both Megan and I played in the Albion College Jazz Band. I wanted so bad to soar into fame and glory like Wynton Marsalis. I wanted to play lead trumpet, I wanted to play all the solos, I wanted so desperately for other people to recognize the genius performer I really was! One morning during our Jazz Band practice, Mr. Miley, our conductor, asked if anyone wanted to play a solo in the piece we were rehearsing. I thought, "Are you kidding?! Why don't you just ask me to play the solo?!" In my pride, I became quiet and despondent as others in the group volunteered to play a solo in the piece. I was fuming inside! Next, Mr. Miley asked everyone to march along for fun, while we played the swinging jazz standard. I noticeably refused. Mr. Miley, seeing that I was the only musician not participating, stopped us in the middle of rehearsing the chart and asked me, "Donny, why aren't you marching?" I said smugly, "I don't feel like it." I brought the whole group down with my bad attitude.

Needless to say, Mr. Miley was not pleased with my willful lack of participation. I felt bad and rushed to his office right away after our rehearsal was over to apologize. I had planned to ask if Megan wanted to enter into a "committed relationship" later that day. But, given the severe embarrassment that happened right in front of her, that question would have to wait for another day.

The second major embarrassing event I remember transpiring between Megan and I also happened in a musical setting, in more ways than one. We were sitting together at the baby grand piano in the Kellogg Center, playing some music and visiting. I don't remember what I ate for lunch that day, but I had some serious gas building up in my GI tract. I prayed that it wouldn't slip out with some offensive sound effect, but sure enough, the involuntary process overcame my voluntary disapproval.

I was mortified there and then. I didn't know how to smooth it over, so I just ran out of the Kellogg Center wishing that it never happened. It really wasn't that big of a deal—I mean, who doesn't pass wind now and then? But there sat Megan at the piano, wondering what just happened and if I was coming back. I ran straight to my dorm room to commiserate with my roommates who would reassure me with their uncontrollable laughter.

Practicing the trumpet in the Higman Park Muldoon cottage.

Summit of Stars

Coincidence. What a beautiful word. Two things coinciding, coming together meaningfully and unpredictably. Perhaps this word has suffered a loss of meaningfulness in our culture as it tends to signify what is random that would otherwise be meaningful. But whenever something happens which we might call "coincidence," it usually means that something meaningful has happened which was outside of our control and yet comes to us as if something else were in control all along.

When I attended student orientation at Albion College, I was placed in the "star" group. Our symbol was a shooting star, and I thought to myself,

"Fitting, as I am quite the football star!" Little did I know that this placement would take on even greater meaning over the course of time.

In spite of my immaturity and shenanigans in my relationship with Megan, we enjoyed so many wonderful times together. We became close friends due to our common interests in music, nature, and our faith. She confided in me early on in our relationship. One important conversation was when she made it a point to talk to me about her parents' recent separation. She poured out her heart and soul and tears to me as I listened and tried to provide some kind of consolation.

One of our favorite spots on campus was the Whitehouse Nature Center. It was an idyllic space filled with hiking trails and so much natural beauty. It bordered the football practice fields and became a coveted place for prayer and contemplation. On one occasion, Megan and a couple of her roommates invited me to come with them to go stargazing out on the practice field next to the nature center. They prevailed upon me and it was a breathtaking experience. It's incredible how many shooting stars you see when you gaze at the nighttime sky for a while. This became a routine of ours and sometimes I would listen to jazz music on my cassette Walkman. I remember listening to the sweet sounds of jazz clarinetist, Sydney Bechet, and wondering if I was crossing the threshold of heaven.

Sometimes Megan and I would go stargazing, just the two of us, and it was great. We always had so much to talk about and so often enjoyed the nighttime silence together. One night, we decided to run around the track in the dark and I remember plunging my foot right into a mud hole, way past my ankle!

Megan and I liked to take risks together too. The Goodrich Chapel was a great place to do so. It had a high-reaching bell tower which housed a few of the music faculty offices. Megan and I decided to take a chance late one evening and climb to the top of the bell tower. No one was around, so we ascended to the top of the tower through a series of elevators and staircases. Finally, we reached the summit—a dark room with a ladder that stretched up to a hatch in the roof that would open right beneath the bell. It was a beautiful experience and yet symbolized so much more.

A picture I drew of Megan and I gazing at the stars on the football practice field during our time at Albion College.

Adding Notes

While at Albion College, I played trumpet in symphonic band, jazz band, and classical orchestra. Myron McReynolds conducted the symphonic band and he took it quite seriously. He loved his profession and it was a joy to play in his ensemble. As I continued to be influenced by jazz music and the art of improvisation, I began to experiment with improvising while playing my part in the symphonic band. Oftentimes, it was subtle and went unnoticed. I thought my added notes enhanced the sound of the music, so I didn't hesitate to make my creative contributions—even in our concerts!

On the Monday following one of our weekend concerts, I was in the music building when Mr. McReynolds invited me into his office. I thought the concert had gone well and I expected that he invited me in to thank me for my fine playing and to express his satisfaction with the performance.

Instead, he asked me with a sharp tone in his voice: "Were you adding notes during the concert?" "Yes," I said. He then went on to scold me about the inappropriateness, pretentiousness, and audacity of doing such a thing. Then he said, "Get out!" And I left his office at once.

Saint Ignace

During the summer of 1998, I served as a middle school camp counselor at Interlochen Fine Arts Camp, near Traverse City, Michigan. It was a wonderful environment in which I was surrounded by top-caliber music and where I could continue to hone my crafts of trumpet-playing and preparing for the upcoming football season at Albion College.

I was very disciplined with my time. I would wake up at 4:30 in the morning to drive down to the gym in Traverse City so that I could get in my intense weight-training for the day. My strength improved dramatically over those summer months. That fall, I would bench press 225 lbs. eleven times in a row at our team's speed and strength testing day at the beginning of the season.

In addition to reading the Bible, practicing the trumpet, football training, and enjoying black cherry ice cream, my heart became more and more occupied with Megan Joanna Nelson. Our friendship continued to blossom as we wrote letters back and forth to each other and talked on the phone. At the end of one of my letters, hoping that Megan would notice what the double entendre implied, I quoted from the Gospel of John, chapter 15: "As the Father loves me, so I also love you. Remain in my love." The truth was that I was falling in love with her and my God at the same time.

Megan and I met up at the McDonald's in Saint Ignace to go walk along the waterfalls there during one of my days off. We got some lunch at the McDonald's and got into my '79 Benz to drive to the falls. I turned on the radio, and, sure enough, "our song" came on: "All My Life" by K-Ci & JoJo. We both felt a little embarrassed—but in a good way.

The time together at Saint Ignace was brilliant. She was wearing her yellow polo shirt—yellow was her favorite color—and I was donned in one of my signature plaid button-down shirts. We walked along the falls and then ended up sitting on the shore of Lake Michigan, right where the Brevoort River met up with the lake. It was beautiful and the day remains tattooed on my memory with the permanence of eternity.

"Whale-catcher"

For my junior jury piece at Albion College, I performed George Enescu's 1906 composition for trumpet and piano, *Légende*. The performance went quite well, high notes and all. After I finished playing, the jury faculty committee conducted a short Q&A with the soloist.

Mr. McReynolds asked me about my future plans. I told him and the committee that I try to take one day at a time. They all laughed and agreed that my approach might help to go about life in a carefree way, but at the same time they encouraged me to give a bit more definition to my future goals.

It was at this brief meeting that I remember Dr. Thomas Doran, the music history and piano professor, saying that my name, "Wallenfang," meant "Whale-catcher," derived from the German words *Wal* ("whale") and *Fang* ("catch").

After Further Review, the Play Still Stands

My junior year at Albion College was a decisive one. Football season was solid. I had worked my way up the roster and saw a lot of playing time. I was the starting placeholder and one of the starting wide receivers. One memory I treasure was our contest against the University of Mount Union. I caught several passes that game but took a hit that injured my lower back and hamstring slightly. We lost the game, but that night Megan came by my room and we went for a walk on campus. Even though I was pretty sore, we had a beautiful time together and our friendship continued to grow.

I remember how tough the pre-season practices were. I would come back to my dorm room at night and just sit there in soreness. Yet I recall imagining that I was doing this all for Megan, like it was my job and I was working hard to support her. This was just a glimmer of things to come.

Our football team ended with an almost perfect record—eight wins, one loss (to Mount Union)—and lost to Mount Union in the first round of the playoffs. They would go on to win the NCAA Division III National Championship that year, much like they do about every year. For the 1999 season, I was staged to be a standout wide receiver. It would be my senior year and my final attempt to reach for the NFL. I believed in possibility.

However, as life unfolded that year, I got into music more and more, to the point that all I wanted to do was to pray and to practice the trumpet. I was loving it. As it turns out, I prayerfully decided to discontinue football and to put all my eggs in the music basket. I met with Coach Rundle in his office to tell him my decision. He encouraged me to think about it a little longer. So I did. Then, when I saw him in the cafeteria one day during lunchtime, I gave him a napkin with the following words inscribed on it: "After further review, the play still stands." No more football. Something even better was in store.

Sister in the Beige Sweater

My relationship with Megan continued to grow. We were in jazz band together and would hang out all the time. I loved spending time with her and began to feel moved in the direction of a committed relationship that would discern the call to marriage. The question was, when to pose the question?

In the meantime, Megan had a deep spiritual experience. She went with some of her friends to the local Black Pentecostal Church, John 3:16 Ministries, for one of their Wednesday evening services. During the service, Pastor Kurtz called out: "Sister in the beige sweater." He was inviting Megan to come forward to be prayed over for healing. She began to sob and experienced again the healing touch of Christ that night. She was struggling still with her parents' separation, and it was prayer like this that saw her through that difficult time in her life.

The day was February 24, 1999, my twenty-first birthday. It wasn't at all on my mind to drink a bunch of alcohol. In fact, I've never been attracted to drinking, and, to this day, I don't drink alcohol (save for a few sips of wine at a special dinner here and there). Actually, my beverage of choice is a cherry coke made with grenadine or cherry juice. Anyways, on my twenty-first birthday, all that was on my mind was to talk to Megan about entering a committed relationship. I had wanted to have this conversation with her for a while, and I was hoping that this day would promise a mutual intention to begin to bind ourselves to one another as best friends and life-long companions.

We had the conversation in the side chapel of Goodrich and it was brilliant. One thing I remember Megan saying to me was, "I feel like you complete me." We were in perfect agreement about what this new relationship meant, and from there on out we were faithful to one another. Could it be that this sister in the beige sweater one day would become my bride?

Megan and I following her junior piano recital in the foyer of Goodrich Chapel at Albion College.

Transposition

My big dilemma going into the summer of '99 was whether or not to transfer to a music school with a full-fledged music program. I figured that I could either finish up at Albion and then go for a master's degree in Trumpet Performance somewhere else, or I could transfer to a music school and then potentially not have to earn a master's degree. So, I decided to give Western Michigan University a try. Late in the game, I contacted the trumpet professors there, Dr. Stephen Jones and Scott Thornburg, and set up an audition.

I played for them some of my favorite solo pieces, including the Wynton Marsalis arrangement of "Grand Russian Fantasia," from his 1987 album, *Carnaval*. I was able to showcase a bit of virtuosity and they were impressed. Even though the deadline passed for offering scholarships for incoming performers, they were able to find a way to squeeze me into the program.

I was thrilled! My newly born dream was being realized: to study under and to perform with the highest caliber musicians around. When I told my Mom the news, she said, "You live a charmed life, kid! A charmed life!"

Now, how was I going to tell Megan the news?

My parents and I following my junior trumpet recital in the foyer of Goodrich Chapel at Albion College.

Upper Peninsula Pines

Megan and I met up soon thereafter in Upper Michigan to visit. Other than a run-in with her Mom's German shepherd, Bailey, it was a great visit. The dog pounced on me with fierce barking and growling when Megan and I were walking out the door of her mother's home. It was not a juvenile German shepherd!

On a stunning summer afternoon, Megan and I took a walk on one of the beautiful trails in the Upper Peninsula woods, lined with pines and cedars all around. I told her the news that I would be transferring to Western

Michigan for the fall to pursue a degree in Trumpet Performance. She was happy for me, but saddened at the same time that we wouldn't be seeing each other every day because we would no longer be going to the same school. However, we'd only be about a forty-five-minute drive away, so it wasn't as bad as it could be.

We were confident that if it was God's will for us to get married, it would happen. We believed that we would stay together if it was meant to be according to God's plan. Nevertheless, as a man, it was difficult for me to sort out my allegiance to my profession and my allegiance to Megan. How were the two supposed to go together? This would take time to learn.

Grandma's Wisdom

That summer, I also visited my Grandpa Lee and Grandma Ellen in Iron Mountain, Michigan. I loved to visit them, enjoying Grandpa's vegetable beef soup and Grandma's Mud Duck pie. I also loved playing trumpet along with my Grandma Ellen playing the piano. We played so much music together, and sometimes Grandpa Lee even would break out his clarinet and we'd have a real jam session! They always were so encouraging about what my brother and I were doing.

On this particular summer afternoon, late in the day, I asked my Grandma a pointed question in the living room: "Grandma, how do you know when you have found the person you're supposed to marry?" She immediately smiled, glanced to the side, then looked back at me and said, "When you can't imagine living without them."

These words would remain with me as I continued to contemplate my relationship with Megan Joanna Nelson.

My Grandma Ellen and I outside my Higman Park home on the occasion of the rehearsal dinner for my wedding.

My Grandpa Lee and Grandma Ellen Wallenfang.

CHAPTER 5

GRAPEVINES

Best of Both Worlds

HAVING A HEART FOR youth ministry, I was invited to chaperone a Steubenville High School Youth Conference during the summer of '99. There was a group of twenty-some kids going from my old high school and the surrounding area. Peggy Brown and my Dad were among the other adult chaperones to accompany the teens.

I had never heard of these conferences before, but I was game for anything that had to do with growing closer to God. So I went.

I loved hanging out with teens. They are so fun and so random! They make the world come to life in their fascination over the smallest and seemingly insignificant things. An eight-hour ride in a minivan packed full of teens may not be most people's idea of a good time, but it was for me.

The theme of the conference was "Going Home to My Father's House." Already I was hooked. A couple years prior, I had fallen in love with the song, "My Father's House," by Audio Adrenaline. This theme couldn't be more perfect and meaningful for me.

Taking place for the most part under a gigantic red and white striped outdoor tent, the conference sessions were electrifying. I had never experienced anything like this before within a Catholic context. Praise and worship. Dancing. Singing with all one's might. Hands raised up high in the air, praising God. Dynamic speakers and powerful witness talks. And the sacraments too.

The first night, the MC gave a "cross talk." He passionately narrated the passion of Jesus. Somehow I was moved to tears. It was real—so real. I was in, all in.

Saturday was fueled by guy and girl breakout sessions, large group sessions, meals, and small-group time. Watching my Dad get into it all with such abandon was amazing. Here was a guy who told me a year or two ago that he didn't have a personal relationship with Jesus. All that seemed to be changing before my very eyes.

The climax of the conference happened on Saturday night. With intense praise and worship music, punctuated by periods of thick silence, the Blessed Sacrament—the Eucharist—was exposed and brought among us in procession. I was floored—literally. I was brought to my knees and there I would remain.

Vividly I still remember the monstrance passing right next to me. My eyes locked with the invisible yet visible eyes of Christ in the Eucharist. He was my Lord and Savior, this much I knew. He passed by, yet stayed with me ever since. The power of God embraces all.

On Sunday, the conference wrapped up with Mass and a sending forth. I remember going to receive Christ in the Eucharist at that Mass with even deeper conviction and joy. I couldn't believe that I was experiencing the best of both worlds: the zeal of Evangelical proclamation and the saturating power of Catholic manifestation. Scripture and sacrament. Preaching and adoration. Charismatic praise and orthodox teaching. The best of both worlds.

The ride back home to Michigan was a blast. I happened to pack my guitar. We sang all of the songs we had sung during the conference, even til past midnight in the Browns' driveway. Could it be true that the best of both worlds was possible after all?

A scene from one of the High School Youth Conferences at Franciscan University of Steubenville in the late 1990s.

Destined

Sitting in a practice room at Western Michigan University, holding my trumpet, I looked in the mirror. I was elated. I believed that my dreams of being a great musician and shining bright in the world of *virtuosi* were close at hand. I thanked God for the opportunity to be at Western to hone my talents and to play among the best musicians in the state.

Everything was in front of me. I had only to work hard and to persevere. While growing up, I practiced the trumpet most of the time in my parents' spacious bathroom because of its acoustics and large wall mirror. I would look into the mirror a lot, most of the time quite pleased with the image I saw looking back at me. Me looking at me. The question remained whether Narcissus would give way to a different face not his own.

All That Jazz

WMU was a musician's heaven. It was incredible to be surrounded by so many talented musicians—to be enveloped by sonorous sound in the Dalton Center. I tended to practice the trumpet upwards of six hours a day. When I wasn't practicing music, I was listening to music. I ate, slept, and breathed music. I played both classical and jazz music, but WMU was really the home of jazz.

Through my auditions, I played lead trumpet in the acclaimed Gold Company vocal jazz ensemble, I was chair of the trumpet section in the symphonic band, and I made the cuts for the elite trumpet sections of the jazz orchestra and the classical orchestra. I frequently played solos in all of my ensembles and was improving my playing like never before. It seemed that the sky was the limit and I was beginning to soar.

Every Sunday, I would play trumpet and sing with the choir of Saint Augustine Cathedral. I felt at home in the choir loft and I'm grateful for organist Frank Zajac, who welcomed me to the group with open arms. He was a tremendous musician and he would say to others about my trumpet playing: "He has serious tone!" That was a huge compliment, coming from him.

I delighted in praising the Lord with music. As much as I liked to bring glory to myself, there seemed to be something deeper in me that yearned to bring glory to God as the point of it all. I remember one of our Gold Company concerts that took place at a large Evangelical church somewhere in Michigan. It was a Christmas concert and our music was hot that night. Toward the end of the concert, with all stops pulled, I remember pointing up to the heavens with my finger while leading our band with sizzling notes. I couldn't help but give credit where credit was due.

The 1999–2000 Gold Company crew at Western Michigan University.

Digging

Truth. That's what I was after. Throughout my life, I have been searching for it. I loved to ponder questions of deepest meaning and highest contemplation. Perhaps music was a way I came into contact with truth, as well as goodness and beauty. Not only did I probe for truth in music, but also in books.

Every day presented new questions about life and God. What is the meaning? What is the purpose? What is the truth? I would read many books. I loved to frequent both Catholic and Protestant bookstores, browsing the shelves to no end. And when I browse, I do so exhaustively. I tend to examine every cover of every book—every nook and cranny of every shelf until I have surveyed them all.

I would ask big questions and small ones, even considering the contents of non-Christian religious traditions of the world: Islam, Hinduism, Judaism, Buddhism, Shintoism, and any other tradition that confronted me with its mysterious otherness. I remember one warm and calm evening, departing from the Waldo Library on the campus of Western Michigan University, toting an English translation of the Quran. The sun glistened upon the gold Arabic etchings on the front of the book as I gazed upon the merciful clouds that hung suspended in the tender evening sky.

Now or Never

While studying music at Western Michigan University, I knew that I needed to make a decision concerning Megan's and my relationship. We had begun our committed relationship on February 24, 1999. It was now early September of 1999. She had let me know on several occasions that she was ready to become engaged. Now it was up to me to ask her.

I started to look at engagement rings at a local jewelry shop in Kalamazoo. I found just the right ring: a cathedral mount white gold band with a modest diamond in the center. I bought the ring and it was only a matter of time until the perfect day for proposing to Megan arrived.

Asking Megan to marry me was a huge decision. I knew that it was one of life's most profound decisions. It was somewhat difficult for me to arrive at the point of readiness. Many things spoke meaning and motivation in me as I approached the point of deciding. There was a song by the Christian band, Smalltown Poets, called "Hold It Up to the Light" that especially spoke to me. It was airing on the radio and I would hear it at unusually significant moments as I was discerning what to do. Have you ever had that experience when that most meaningful song comes on the radio at just the right time, and you can't help but believe that God is speaking to you through that song? The song's lyrics addressed me directly. I encourage you to listen to this song and reflect on your own life—even right now. To what is God calling you next? How can you be plunged ever deeper in his sea of infinite mercy, and lead other people to do the same?

The song speaks of "the choice of a lifetime" and not being "too late for that flight." Its meaning crescendoes by proclaiming the truth that "there's no choice at all if I don't make my move, and trust that the timing is right." The choice needs to be held up to the light of the will of God the Father. Is it his will or not? This song helped me not be afraid of the magnitude of this decision. It helped me to realize that if I didn't make my move, the chance of Megan and I marrying might pass us by.

Ultimatum

I searched high and I searched low. I searched near and I searched far. Through it all I realized that truth could not be met with contradictions. Either God is or God is not. Either Jesus is the eternal Son of God or he is not. Either eternal life is real or it is not.

Upon studying the Quran, for example, I was presented with a claim that contradicted that of Christianity. For Islamic belief, Jesus is not the eternal Son of God or consubstantial with God the Father. There is no divine Trinity for Islam. Again, either God is a Trinity of divine Persons or not.

I believed then and I believe now that God has revealed Godself as a Trinity of divine Persons: God the Father, God the Son, and God the Holy Spirit. This truth about God's self-revelation is surely a dividing theological line between Islam and Christianity, and between Christianity and all of the other great religious traditions around the world. While appreciating so many of the beautiful depictions of divinity in the Quran, its overt and explicit denial of the divine sonship of Jesus was a claim I could not accept.

I returned to Waldo Library to make photocopies of those passages in the Quran that disagreed with Christian belief. It was an ultimatum: either Jesus is Lord or he is not. I believe that he is, and the blood he shed on the cross, coupled with his victorious resurrection from the dead, is the most convincing evidence.

Victory Park

The night had arrived. It was September 24, 1999, and I went to visit Megan back in Albion. I've always been an all-or-nothing kind of person, and this night I wanted to put it all on the line for Megan. I had discerned the call to marriage to be the will of God, and on this night the road to marriage would begin definitively.

The moon was shining bright on this impeccably beautiful fall evening. We took a stroll down South Hannah Street, hand in hand, and sat along the bank of the North Branch of the Kalamazoo River, with Sprankle-Sprandel football stadium fading into the shadowy backdrop. I was waiting for the perfect moment to risk the question—no cars passing by, no dogs barking, desiring serene solitary silence. I continued to make sure the engagement ring box was still in the pocket of my Champion cardigan sweatshirt.

After a while, we walked across the street into the heart of Victory Park—the place where I used to do grueling conditioning workouts as an athlete on the Albion College football team; the place where I discerned to change my major from pre-medicine to music; the place where I played my trumpet on the stage of a vacant band shell to an audience of no one. I had my wedding proposal delivery ready, and now I just needed the pristine celestial moment to follow through.

After what seemed like an eternity, we made our way into the middle of an open grassy field, again on the bank of the Kalamazoo River, this time with a gentle water fall purring in the background. This was a special place of prayer to which I would go during my three years of studying at Albion College. There were many mystical encounters experienced in that place, and this night would crescendo to yet another one. I fell to one knee, pulled the engagement ring out of my pocket, raised it in hope and victory to Megan with the following words:

"I had asked my Grandma Ellen, 'How do you know when you have found the person you're supposed to marry?' She said to me, 'When you can't imagine living without them.' Megan, I can't imagine living without you. Will you marry me?" Amidst tears of joy and sniffles, she said, "Yes!"

An aerial shot of Victory Park in Albion, Michigan. Note the heart shape of plants in the very location I asked Megan to marry me.

Balloons and Champagne

There are those moments in life when time seems to stand still. December 31, 1999, was one of those times for me. Many families of the SS John and Bernard faith community gathered that evening to usher in the New Millenium with prayer, worship, thanksgiving and celebration. I played the classic hymn, "Be Still My Soul," on the trumpet, with Megan accompanying on piano, and we played from our hearts. Together we waited in hope for the good things to come in the year 2000 and beyond.

Our wedding date was set for May 27, 2000, at Saint Augustine Cathedral. This was a special year indeed. Y2K! New Year's Eve culminated with a special order of prayer: to write our hopes for the New Year on miniature scrolls and to tie these to helium-filled balloons. We all went outside in the winter evening air and released our balloons simultaneously into the sky when the clock struck midnight.

I don't remember what I wrote on that tiny scroll that night, but I suspect that whatever it was, in some mysterious way, Megan and I are enjoying today the fruits of that tender hope sealed fresh in the midnight hour. After surrendering the balloons and their fragile passengers to the nighttime sky, we headed back inside the church hall for a toast of champagne. Three years prior, the effervescence of champagne bubbled up in me at the Urbana Conference in Urbana-Champaign, Illinois. On this night become early morning, the elixir circulated once again, quieting my disquieted heart—stilling my restless soul—on the shores of incandescent virgin futures.

Forensics and Flubs

Looking back at my time at Western Michigan University, there were many successes—and, of course, some failures along the way too. With all the talent that I self-touted, could you believe that I tended to be afraid to perform—too nervous to take the stage? I would get so nervous that I always toted a cup of water with me during performances because my mouth would get so dry. I would dodge opportunities to play at department recitals because I was worried about not playing perfectly.

I often would practice so much each day that, for some auditions and performances, my embouchure would be too fatigued to play well. My "lops would be chopped," as we used to say! For example, in the master class when Dr. Jones let me play his Schilke piccolo trumpet, I struggled to get the notes out just right. Or the audition when my fellow trumpeter, Adam, asked what piece I was going to play, and I said, "The Carnival of Venice," and he responded, "You're going to blow us all out of the water!" Yet, I remember drowning in my own disappointment at how the audition went. I was always so afraid to miss notes and I let that get in the way of playing with reckless abandon.

The truth is that we miss 100 percent of the notes that we don't play. You just have to go for it and risk being human! We aren't robots after all, but hazardous humans that only can give it our best shot and not worry about how the chips fall, as long as we are living with resolute responsibility for the other.

Overall, I gradually overcame most of my fears of failing, and I tended to perform with excellence. When my parents came to my performances, they would be beaming with pride. One such performance was in Miller Auditorium, in front of a packed crowd. The show began with a brass musical composition and a rising stage. It was awesome! There I was next to Dr. Stephen Jones, my trumpet professor, in tuxedoes, as the stage rose up from the underground and we magically appeared in front of the audience. There were my Mom, Dad, and Megan sitting stage right, glowing with joy at their beloved in his glory.

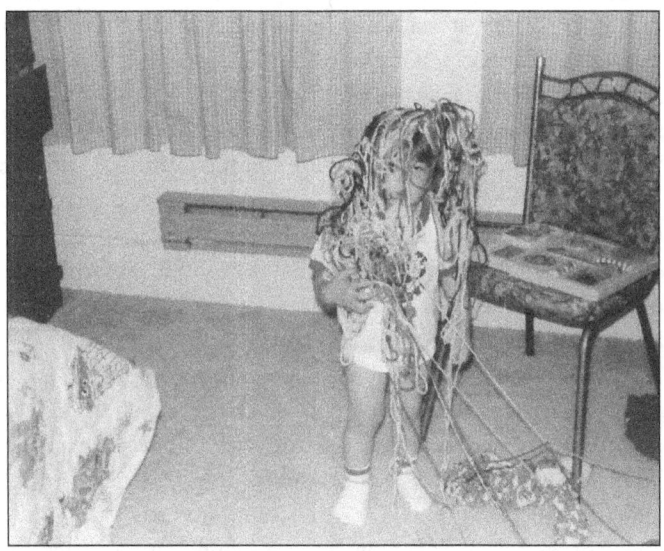

Me having a yarn overdose at a young age.

Another Wallenfang family Christmas jam session.

Self-abandonment

The most monumental day of my life was May 27, 2000. It was my wedding day. Megan and I finally were getting married. In preparation for this day, 150 days before, we would read one psalm each day from the Book of Psalms in the Bible, beginning with Psalm 150 and ending with Psalm 1 on the morning of May 27. It was a way for us to count down the days prayerfully and with great anticipation.

The event of our marriage took place at Saint Augustine Cathedral in Kalamazoo, Michigan, at ten o'clock on a Saturday morning. We had a lot of recent history there with our participation in the Cathedral choir and our part-time work in leading the school liturgical music and youth ministry. Wherever we were, we were all in.

Megan and I both knew what this day was about: giving ourselves totally to one another for the rest of our lives, and seeking the will of God the Father, not by ourselves any longer, but together.

Megan and I thought it would be appropriate if my parents walked me down the aisle first, and then her parents walked her down the aisle second. As I was preparing to be escorted down the aisle, I noticed my little cousin, Tyler, in his little black tuxedo. I then looked down the aisle and up above the altar at the crucifix with the Blessed Virgin Mary and Saint John standing below. I began to cry. This moment was a culmination of my entire life and its definitive meaning came into sharp relief: to abandon yourself and to give yourself away. Just like Jesus, I understood this nuptial liturgy to signify a complete offering of self, one-for-the-other. The Bridegroom was being called to lay down his life for his Bride (see Eph 5:25).

A torrential rain poured over us as we exited the cathedral following our wedding liturgy, and we could not help but interpret it as a sign of great blessing.

Pictures from our wedding on May 27, 2000, in Saint Augustine Cathedral, Kalamazoo, Michigan.

Grapevines

Southwest Michigan is known to be a "fruit-belt" region of sorts. Apple orchards, grape vineyards, and blueberry patches checker Berrien county, and, during harvest season, you can smell the sweetness of the various fruits while driving down the country roads. Megan and I thought it only natural to honeymoon on the shores of Lake Michigan. We actually had no definite plans—just a drive to the southwest coast, find a nice restaurant and place to stay for the night. We ended up encountering and eating at Amicarelli Vineyard Restaurant in South Haven. I'm always on the lookout for meaningfulness in words and names, and the name of this particular restaurant, in its own way, served to confirm the divine appointment of our marital vocation: friendship and fruitfulness.

On the inside of our wedding rings, before the day of our wedding, Megan and I had "John 15" inscribed. It was in reference to the Gospel reading of our wedding liturgy and a biblical text that spoke to us even during the early stages of our friendship:

> I am the true vine, and my Father is the vine grower. He takes away every branch in me that does not bear fruit, and every one that does he prunes so that it bears more fruit—Remain in me as I remain in you—I am the vine, you are the branches—As the Father loves me, so I also love you. Remain in my love—I have told you this so that my joy may be in you and your joy may be complete. This is my commandment: love one another as I love you.

Here we were on our honeymoon with these meanings reverberating around us again: friendship and fruitfulness. The symbol of grapes on the vine would continue to turn up throughout our life of marriage, always reminding us of the power of God at work within our sacramental unity of diversified persons.

The morning after the consummation of our marriage, Megan and I attended Mass with my parents at the church in which I was raised: Saint John the Evangelist in Benton Harbor, Michigan. I played trumpet in the choir loft in praise of what God was doing in our young lives. No rest for the blessed!

Husband and wife. May 27, 2000.

Left Behind

On Saturday, April 22, 2000, Megan had entered the Catholic Church. She was raised in a variety of Protestant settings—Mennonite, Presbyterian, Assembly of God, and Episcopal. Even before becoming engaged, in that side chapel of Goodrich, we had talked about wanting to seek the truth together, concerning things about God and life. Both of us were open to pursuing the fullness of truth, wherever that might lead us.

About a month after our wedding, we were scheduled to serve as chaperones for a group of high school students from Southwest Michigan going to a Steubenville Youth Conference in Ohio. I had chaperoned this retreat weekend a year before and it had revolutionized my faith and taught me what was possible for Catholic Christianity in relation to Protestant Christianity. There I really discovered the best of both worlds.

The morning we woke up to set out on the trip, I could tell that my body wasn't feeling well. I was nervous. A couple hours later we began our drive east, in a van full of teenagers, with Megan at the wheel. Only minutes into the trip, I began vomiting in a bag. At our first stop, I found myself fastened to a toilet seat in a church bathroom, with fluids escaping my body in every direction! My Mom had to come pick me up and Megan ventured onward with my Dad, other chaperones, and a group of lively teens.

It turns out that this would be an important time of empowerment in her own faith, even apart from me. She, too, would witness the possibility of the truth of Catholicism met with the zeal and joy through attentiveness to Scripture, preaching, worship, and testimony as exemplified by Protestant Christianity.

Refinement

During our first year of marriage, Megan and I both attended Western Michigan University, completing our bachelor's degrees in music. She began to pursue studies in music therapy, while I wrapped up a highly employable degree in trumpet performance. We were living on prayer, love, music, and government cheese!

My musical interests continued to evolve, and I began to focus on classical and church music. I aimed at producing the purest tone possible, and my trumpet professors and fellow musicians were quite impressed. People would say that it sounded like I was singing through the horn. It seemed like I was chiseling away at a masterpiece, refining the work by removing any unnecessary dross and thereby arriving at what was most essential. I especially was listening to recordings of Maurice André, whose buttery tone impressed me the most.

At the same time, when one becomes obsessed with developing a masterpiece, so fixated on refining and concentrating a work of art, there emerges the unintended effect of inattentiveness in relation to other people, including those closest to you. Sometime early on, while Megan and

I were finishing our final year of undergraduate studies, she let me know gently in a conversation at our Stuart Avenue apartment that it seemed that I loved two things, and one of them was not her. The two things I loved, in her view, were God and music. I took her words to heart immediately, apologized, and began to work at being much more attentive to her and balancing all of the various facets of life.

Labor Pains

Our first year of marriage was wonderful. In addition to our studies in music at Western Michigan University, we were very active at Saint Augustine Cathedral in music and youth ministry. I even worked part-time in maintenance at the parish during the summer of 2000. Megan worked for an organization that served people with severe developmental disabilities, honing her craft of music therapy in profound ways.

Our first child, Ellen Agnes (named after her grandmothers, Ellen and Ellen, and her great grandmother, Agnes), was conceived in August of 2000. Less than one year after our engagement, our first child came into being—the greatest fruit of this intermingling of divine and human love. Megan experienced significant bouts of morning sickness, vomiting at around 10:30 every morning. We began to joke that there must be a spit-fire red-head in her womb, and this was not far from the truth.

Nearing graduation, I had no job lined up, but not a little trust in the Lord. My Mom left a phone message to let me know of a youth ministry job opening in my hometown area of Saint Joseph, Michigan. Saint Joseph Catholic Church was looking to hire someone to start up a LifeTeen program—a dynamic youth ministry that featured contemporary worship music at a Sunday evening liturgy. At first, I was a bit skeptical of the opening, but I warmed up to it after a while.

I had begun to take guitar lessons when I was twelve years old and I increased my proficiency on guitar at Albion College when helping to lead worship at our InterVarsity and Fellowship of Christian Athletes meetings. I certainly could lead worship for the LifeTeen youth ministry program and was a serious candidate for this position, even without a degree in theology.

In the meantime, at the beginning of April 2001, I was scheduled to have hernia surgery (a condition I probably developed from all the weightlifting for football, as well as all of the exertion of the lower viscera in trumpet playing), I had no job secured, and I would not be able to play the trumpet for a while. On top of all this, Ellen was due to be born at the end of the month. It was rather stressful, hoping that all of the necessary pieces would fall into place, but, fortunately, Megan and I had the constant support of our parents through it all.

I even ended up making an appointment at a local employment agency, remaining open to any kind of work, manual or clerical. Weeks went by with no call from the employment agency. I got an interview for the youth ministry position at Saint Joseph Catholic Church, but weeks went by without a callback from them either.

CHAPTER 6 ──────────────

PLAYGROUND OF LIFE

Crossing the Threshold

NOTHING MAKES YOU FORGET yourself like having a child. Conceiving Ellen Agnes (a name meaning "light" and "lamb") was cause for great transcendence. I remember on some day after Ellen had been conceived, driving in my car, shifting my eyes back and forth between the road and the clouds. It was a sort of ecstatic experience, marveling at the miraculousness of life and contemplating the profundity of becoming a father. Who was this little one, and who should I be for her?

Tremendous delight surged within my heart, and I couldn't help but to thank God in a constant way, praying for the health and well-being of Ellen and praising God for the gift he had bestowed upon Megan and me. We sensed that we were "crossing the threshold into the greatest responsibility." Ellen was born on April 30, 2001, in Kalamazoo, Michigan. There emerged the spit-fire red-head into the light of day, and life never would be the same for Megan and me—but happily so. A vivid poem of Saint John Paul II, called "Pre-sacrament," sums up well the vocation to motherhood and fatherhood. The end of it reads:

> Pre-sacrament—existence itself as the outward sign of
> eternal Love.
> And when they become "one flesh"
> —that wondrous union—
> on the horizon there appears the mystery of
> fatherhood and motherhood.
> —They return to the source of life within them.
> —They return to the Beginning.
> —Adam knew his wife

and she conceived and gave birth.
They know they have crossed the threshold
of the greatest responsibility![1]

Pictures of Megan, Ellen and I.

---

1. John Paul II, *Roman Triptych: Meditations*, translated by Jerzy Peterkiewicz (Washington, DC: United States Council of Catholic Bishops, 2003) 20–21.

Boyz II Men

One of my favorite R&B groups while growing up was Boyz II Men. As a vocal ensemble, their music was so rich with harmonies, so sonorous and soothing! The name of their group would take on new meaning as I became a husband and father. I indeed was changing from a boy to a man. Needing to work a full-time job, trying to get health insurance, paying many bills, and pouring myself out for Megan and Ellen became my daily purpose.

It was liberating that any kind of personal dreams and ambitions gave way to my new dream that had become a daily reality: Megan and Ellen, "my girls." I just wanted to be with them as much as possible every single day. I loved to hold Ellen, watch her sleep, and contemplate the meaning of her infancy. Because of her, I understood much better my relationship with God the Father, my creator. I was his beloved child, and nothing could change that fundamental fact of my existence.

Fishing for Teens

The days were passing by and I still had not heard word from Saint Joseph Catholic Church. Finally, around mid-May 2001, I called up Fr. Eugene Sears to ask if the search committee had made a decision concerning my candidacy for this youth minister position. He said they had come to a decision and would like to offer me the job for an annual salary of $23,000 plus benefits. I was elated! I accepted the job right way. After I hung up the phone, I announced the good news to Megan and I jumped up and touched the ceiling of our little cottage, nestled in the valley of Higman Park, on the shores of Lake Michigan.

Through my experiences at Albion College and in Kalamazoo, I came to sense that the Lord was calling me to be his witness. In addition to my family life, my one desire was to give glory to him by leading other people to a lasting encounter with his merciful love. Serving in full-time ministry in the Catholic Church allowed me to invest my gifts directly in the lives of teenagers. I had a great love for young people and yearned for them to encounter the living God with passion and power. Steubenville youth conferences and LifeTeen were movements in the Catholic Church that incorporated a more charismatic approach to worship and ministry and capitalized on the natural vibrancy and electricity of teens. Given my dull and rather dead experience of going to Mass every week growing up, I believed that this energized missionary approach was essential to draw young people deeper into the Church and the fullness of God the Father's revelation in his Son, Jesus Christ.

While I'm not able to recount all that happened during those two-and-a-half years of youth ministry that I led at Saint Joseph Catholic Church, I can attest that it was beautiful. Hundreds of teens were involved in this ministry, and the sight of 100+ teens overflowing around the altar during the Eucharistic prayer during the Sunday evening Mass was awe-inspiring. God the Holy Spirit was on the move, and it gave me unbounded joy to serve to mediate this movement of grace among us:

> These things will I remember
> as I pour out my soul:
> how I would lead the rejoicing crowd
> into the house of God,
> amid cries of gladness and thanksgiving,
> the throng wild with joy. (Ps 42:5)

I resonated with the LifeTeen approach to youth ministry: earn the right to be heard and meet teens where they're at so as to bring them closer to Christ. My eyes always were set on the margins. Trying to follow the ways of Jesus, the Good Shepherd, I would seek out the one kid sitting alone, the awkward girl who doesn't fit in, the mysterious and even frightening teen in all-black Gothic dress with piercings whose home life is in shambles, the young person who is a racial minority, the boy with disabilities that many people seem to avoid. Cast the net far and wide and gather up everything in between. This missionary approach to ministry was in my bones, and I knew that I was right where God wanted me to be. Even my Dad, John, was a member of our youth ministry Core team during those years at Saint Joseph Catholic Church.

Pure Tone

Throughout my studies in trumpet performance at Western Michigan University, I worked and worked to develop the purest sound possible on the trumpet. Many people commented on how it sounded like I "sang through the horn." I ended up turning my attention away from jazz playing and focused exclusively on classical and church playing. I concentrated the sound so much to the point that even the instrument itself seemed to get in the way of the transcendent purity at which I took aim.

Following my new youth ministry job, and recovery from hernia surgery, I began to practice the trumpet again and perform here and there. I even resumed practicing the virtuosic solo for piccolo trumpet in Bach's *Brandenburg Concerto, No. 2*! Yet, one morning, when I was practicing the trumpet in the choir loft of Saint Joseph Catholic Church, I suddenly stopped playing. I felt like the Holy Spirit was moving me to put the trumpet down and spend all of my time with my family and in youth ministry activities.

All of a sudden, the trumpet seemed unnatural and an obstacle to the pure sonority for which I yearned. I had developed my trumpet playing to a professional degree, and I felt that I either had to maintain that advanced degree of performance, practicing at least two hours every day, or I couldn't play at all. My all-or-nothing-personality was coming through once again!

From that day forward I never really played the trumpet again. I ended up selling all of my trumpets back to the store in South Bend where they were purchased originally. The trumpet, too, I laid down on the altar of sacrifice for the sake of a purity that I eventually would find only in the silence of contemplative prayer on the high solitary altitudes of Mount Carmel.

Pentecost Hair

Conceiving a child or adopting a child is a gift. The child is a gift to his or her mother and father and to the world. One of the great limitations of this book is that I inevitably must leave out so many precious details about the lives of my children as I have observed them over the years. I do this for the sake of making a shorter and more pointed narrative, but I do so with great regret.

Gift is one of the best words to describe the child because every day he or she comes to you as an incredible gift. Their beauty, their littleness, their innocence, their posture of wonder facing the world, their witness to the creativity and finesse of the God who made us, their testimony of the boundless love of a Father who keeps his promises.

If you have ever spent time with a child, you know what I'm talking about. One of the most nefarious lies is that the child is a burden. No, the child is a burden only to the self-absorbed gluttonous self who has not yet discovered his true vocation: to live in love and responsibility for the other person who faces him. If there is one thing that I want my epitaph to read, it is: he was a faithful husband and father. The whole of my life—that which is of greatest substance and value—could be summed up in the gift of the child, my vocation in relation to the child, and, thereby, in relation to the entire world. There is no accomplishment, no book, no accolade or award, no possession or enjoyment, in comparison to the incomparable gift of the child, and spending as much time with the personal gift as possible, letting him and her give themselves in their glory to their undeserving witness and beloved beneficiary.

Again, this book is entitled *iGod* because it seeks to tell the story of that self-absorbed gluttonous self who discovered his true vocation: an iGod turned inside out. The orientation changes from iGod to God–You, in which yielding to the other to the point of abandonment is the perfection of human living.

Just over a year after Ellen was born, our son, Aubin Augustine, was conceived. We named him after Saint Albinus (Aubin) of Angers and Saint Augustine. Megan and I liked unique and uncommon names, and this was one of them. Aubin was born on March 22, 2003, in Saint Joseph, Michigan. Shortly after he was born, he was diagnosed with transient tachypnea, which is a condition in which the infant's lungs are still underdeveloped. In addition, the pediatric doctor was concerned that Aubin's heart also was not fully developed for his age, so he was taken by ambulance to Bronson Methodist Hospital in Kalamazoo, the same hospital where Ellen had been born. Aubin would stay there in the NICU for one whole week before he was allowed to go home. This was a trying time as parents, not knowing what exactly was happening or what was going to happen.

Megan and I were so thankful when Aubin eventually came home. We marveled at his bright red hair that would stand up on end when he would wake up in the morning from a good night's sleep. We called him "Pentecost hair" because it looked like there were tongues of fire dancing on his soft little head. The threshold of the greatest responsibility was redoubled, but Megan and I were up for the gift and the challenge.

Megan, Ellen, Aubin, and I at Aubin's baptism in Saint Joseph Catholic Church in Saint Joseph, Michigan, the same church where my high school Baccalaureate event took place, and where I served as youth minister for my first job.

Johnny U

I loved my Dad and he loved me. He and my Mom raised me to have a deep passion for the Catholic faith, academics, sports, and music. I worked very hard at all I did in order to make my parents proud. I looked up to my Dad since childhood. I would learn about the things he did growing up and I would want to emulate him in every way. He was a straight-A student. I wanted to be a straight-A student. He was class president. I wanted to be class president. He played the trumpet. I wanted to play the trumpet.

He was quarterback of the football team. I wanted to be quarterback of the football team. When he played high school football for the Niagara Badgers, he wore number 19—the same number as his favorite NFL quarterback, Johnny Unitas. Though I would end up wearing number 3, as my dream crystalized facing the golden dome of Our Lady's university, everything I did was fueled by the model I had in my Dad.

Pictures of my father, John Wallenfang, both during his high school football days with the Niagara Badgers (wearing number 19), and later as a football coach for the Lake Michigan Catholic Lakers.

He became our head football coach when I was in eighth grade. Though we won no games that season, I never gave up hope that the Laker tide would change current at some point, and our team would win more games than we would lose. My Dad remained an assistant football coach throughout my and my brother, Mike's, high school years. He played so many hours of catch with us in the front yard and always made himself available when we asked him to come out and play with us. A vivid memory stands out of him tying his sneakers, which was the unshakable sign that he was about to come outside and throw the ball.

Even after I graduated from Western Michigan University and moved back to my hometown, my Dad offered his time and energy in the youth ministry program I was directing. He, too, had chaperoned the Steubenville Youth Conferences and was growing leaps and bounds in his life of faith. His favorite worship song was "Agnus Dei" by Third Day. At that time, he also took up his baritone again and was playing in the local community band.

My Dad had a deep German soul that loved good beer, good jokes, critical academic questions, and a wild game of football. *Genuß. Schmeckt gut.*

I remember one day my Mom calling me and asking Megan and I to come over to their house that evening because they wanted to talk with us about something. I was a little nervous as we pulled into their driveway and got out of the car. I could see and hear my Dad practicing his baritone inside their house. He seemed like a child, doing something that he enjoyed. My Dad always was young at heart—a jokester—playful and full of good humor at every turn. He never lost the lighter side of life, full of joy, mischief, and savor of the simple pleasures that life affords.

The somber meeting began by my Mom and Dad telling us that he had test results come back and he was diagnosed with malignant colon cancer that had most likely metastasized to other places in his body. He soon would have a surgical biopsy done on his liver. I was there in the hospital waiting during his surgery; there when the surgeon came to tell my Mom, my brother and I the bad news; there in my Dad's hospital room when he woke up after surgery and asked me if they found cancer in his liver. I told him that they had, but immediately tried to give him hope that there were some promising treatments being developed that might work to keep the cancer at bay.

My brother and I left the hospital together and talked for a bit in the parking lot. I said to him, "This isn't just Dad's cancer. This is our cancer." We both knew that we would never cease to live in solidarity with our father until the day he died. Together we vowed to be with him and care for him to the end. I was twenty-four and my brother, Mike, was twenty-two.

My father's high school senior picture.

Playground of Life

Throughout the next year, my Dad underwent many rounds of chemotherapy. As his liver continued to fail, his skin turned yellow and began to itch. I remember one night when I had to stay at his house and help him to the bathroom multiple times as he coughed up blood. He was so weak from his chemo and blood thinner. It felt like we were on a boat that was sinking, and all we could do was to keep bailing out water to stay afloat for as long as possible.

About a year after being diagnosed with stage-four liver cancer, my Dad, my two-year-old daughter, Ellen, and I walked down to a children's park together. We were the only ones there. As Ellen played joyfully on the playground equipment, my Dad and I talked about life. He was thinking about dying. I said to him, "But, Dad, you'll get to see Jesus." He said in reply, "But why now?" as he sat down at the bottom of a slide and began to weep. He was thinking about all the life he would seem to miss out on, such as watching his grandkids grow up.

My Mom and Dad at my Dad's retirement celebration at Lake Michigan College during the fall of 2001.

My Dad and I, golfing with several of his friends from church during the summer of 2001.

Fishing at Night

While growing up, my Dad took my brother, Mike, and I on several fishing trips on small inland lakes. One trip involved travelling all the way around Lake Michigan and making fishing stops on inland lakes along the way. During this trip, we arrived at one of our fishing destinations, and, for some reason, we were missing one fishing pole. My Dad volunteered to be the one to go without a pole, but then he found a nice, sturdy stick and tied fishing line around it. He ended up catching way more fish than the rest of us with his makeshift fishing rod! I was so jealous! My Dad was not a burly outdoorsman, but he did things like this with Mike and I because he loved spending time with us.

Fast-forward to another expedition—this time, a mystical one. The date was December 1, 2003. I had visited with my parents earlier in the day at their home. My Mom had cooked homemade vegetable beef soup—a dish we affectionately called "Grandpa Lee's Soup," named after my father's Dad, Lee Wallenfang. He used to make this soup and enjoy it very much. My Dad usually enjoyed it too, but not today. He had recently gone on hospice and was especially tired.

He had been napping on the couch throughout the day, but he stayed awake long enough to talk with me about a new job opportunity that might be coming my way in Wisconsin, the state in which he was born and raised. It was in the Diocese of Green Bay and this place of course called to mind the Green Bay Packers, my Dad's favorite team. I told him about this new job opening, that it would pay $10,000 more than my current job, and that I would get to do more focused religious education. It seemed like a good fit. He told me, "Donny, it clearly is the better choice." With that blessing, I shortly said goodbye, told him I loved him, and went back to my house.

A couple hours later, my Mom called me at home. She was crying. She said that my Dad was laying on the couch and was breathing, but not responding. I went back over to their house. My brother, Mike, and Jim and Cynda Muldoon came over too. My Dad was on the doorstep of death and we all knew it.

My Dad on the edge of the battlefields of Gettysburg, Pennsylvania. He took a trip there with his brother, Ron, during the final year of his life. These pictures of my Dad and his umbrella are symbolic of his fight with the storm of cancer that came as a surprise during the golden years of his life.

Father Bill Jacobs, pastor of Saints John and Bernard Catholic Church, came to anoint my Dad one final time with the Sacrament of the Sick. He stayed for a while, keeping vigil with us at the side of the couch. My Dad occasionally would let out a faint moan, but he clearly was too tired to talk.

We transferred him to a hospice bed that was wheeled in the living room. It seemed like his throat began to fill with mucus, and I tried the best I could to clear it away from his mouth. Suddenly, my Dad's body arched backward, the back of his throat began to bubble, and I think Mike and I, who were standing at either side, both said "shit" (the word came out as involuntarily as his soul left his body), and we began to weep profusely while hugging and kissing the un-ensouled body of our father. Immediately I recognized the precise meaning of King Hezekiah's prayer:

> In the noontime of life I said, I must depart! To the gates of Sheol I have been consigned for the rest of my years. I said, I shall see the LORD no more in the land of the living. Nor look on any mortals among those who dwell in the world. My dwelling, like a shepherd's tent, is struck down and borne away from me; you have folded up my life, like a weaver who severs me from the last thread. From morning to night you make an end of me; I cry out even until the dawn. Like a lion he breaks all my bones; from morning to night you make an end of me. Like a swallow I chirp; I moan like a dove. My eyes grow weary looking heavenward: LORD, I am overwhelmed; go security for me! (Isa 38:10–14)

After the undertakers came to bring our father's body to the funeral home, I drove home in silence, stupefied at what just happened. I told Megan and she cried and consoled me. I couldn't sleep, of course, so I listed to a few songs that I had on CDs. One song, "Word of God Speak," was by MercyMe, and another one, "I Still Believe," was by Jeremy Camp. The song "I Still Believe" repeats the refrain: "Even when I don't see, I still believe." I knew that I needed to exercise this faith beyond seeing now more than ever.

My Dad tossing me up and catching me in the waters of Lake Michigan.

Morning Glory

The next morning, Megan took our kids, Ellen and Aubin, with her to a Bible study down the street, to give me some time to be by myself. I sat at the piano and played a few songs. One was an original composition that I never named. Playing this song made me feel great thanksgiving for my Dad, the life he gave me through adoption, and all of the times we shared together.

I began to weep, both in thanksgiving and in sorrow. Life would never be the same without him, and I was just beginning to understand what that meant.

Though my Mom was now a widow, I had to provide for my family, and a new job on the other side of Lake Michigan beckoned. I felt that the Lord was calling us there and I also had my Mom's blessing to go.

The name of the church was Saint Peter the Fisherman. It was a beautiful name in a beautiful place. God confirmed this change of job with many accompanying signs—for example, the signs on the highway ("Peterbuilt," "Petro"), the red and white minivans in the interview parking lot, parked side-by-side, signifying Divine Mercy and the blood and water that flowed from the side of Christ, the grapevine stenciling in the kitchen and the two large fish we found in the freezer of our new home on Waldo Boulevard in Manitowoc. When a person enters into contemplative prayer, everything lights up with meaning and God speaks clearly to the soul who trusts in him.

Paying Dues

As you could expect, my new job had its highs and its lows, and, if the truth be told, it probably had more lows than highs. It is not what you hope for in a new job. Rather, you would like your new job to be next to perfect if at all possible. But the fact was that I was young, relatively inexperienced, naïve, gentle, incredibly joyful, and fairly uneducated "on paper" for what I was hired to do. I had a bachelor's degree in trumpet performance and yet was working in full-time religious education and youth ministry in the Catholic Church. Looking back, I feel like some people leveraged all of my apparent inadequacies against me, even though I tended to do good work and had a whole lot of love, energy, vision, and knowledge about the faith.

It is doubly difficult when you have a family to support and you can't just quit your job and find another one easily. There were times when I was demeaned and berated, got yelled at (for doing nothing wrong, like moving music stands from one building to another or trying to line up a priest for a retreat), brought to tears in my office, and was made to feel like Cinderella, confined to a bed of ashes and an 8–5 work day with an hour break for lunch, while the world was wasting away, waiting for deeper encounter with the Savior and his Church to reach out to them.

I remember feeling such anxiety at that job. Like preparing for the confirmation liturgy with the bishop. It seemed like I had a list of a-million-and-one things to do, and, as my predecessor warned me, "I would be crucified" if I did not do them perfectly. Like having the lemons ready for the bishop to wash the chrism oil off of his hands during the liturgy, or ordering the fish to serve at the reception, or taking out the "smokey joe's" for a reconciliation service. In a word, humiliation.

Yet the Lord teaches us many things through our involuntary experiences of humiliation. I knew that I had to pay my dues, and, if God's will be done, grow in virtue. I remember one very difficult day at work, coming home and looking at the dining room table, feeling the weight of the world on my shoulders and knowing that I couldn't just up and quit my job. Even though I felt sick to my stomach, I had to stick it out and pray that God would make a way out of no way.

One of the great blessings that happened came out of necessity. Because I did not have any official academic training in theology, I was told that I needed either to do the three-year diocesan certification program in catechesis or complete a master's degree in theological studies through Saint Norbert College. I chose the latter, again out of necessity, and I was welcomed into a world of learning that I came to love greatly.

Even though the job was challenging overall, the ministry had a fruitfulness about it. By the grace of God, we started an outreach ministry called The Wharf. I served as the master catechist for the weekly high school catechesis program and confirmation preparation. Also, I served as band leader of our worship team for the Sunday evening liturgy. I developed media presentations, small group questions, and tried to create an environment in which young people could encounter the risen Christ like never before. I was being empowered in ways that I didn't expect, even if I had to learn through "the school of hard knocks."

Every night of our weekly large-group gathering of teens, I would play prerecorded music as they arrived. I always began with the song "Gone Fishin'" by a band called Stellar Kart. The song relates the vocation of becoming "a fisher of men" as a disciple of Jesus Christ. "If anybody needs me, tell them I've gone fishin'—Jesus is the only way, that's why I've gone fishin'."

This was an interesting parish situation—a small town that once upon a time was home to four different Catholic ethnic parishes now all merged into one. The community was about to break ground to build a brand-new church when I arrived. One of the old churches became a workout facility and another one was demolished, and a Walgreens was put up in its place. To say the least, I entered this new job setting in the midst of not a little turmoil.

God Is Good

My wife, Megan, and I began to develop a saying upon conceiving our third child: "new job, new house, new baby!" This became the steady trend for us over the years. Our third child we named Tobias Xavier. Tobias is a name that means "YHWH is good" and Xavier means "bright, splendid, and new house." Francis Xavier was my confirmation name, as well as a family name (I had a great grandfather Francis Xavier Wallenfang), and so Xavier had significance with respect to those connections too.

Toby was a beautiful child—a great blessing in the storm. He renewed our joy all the more and was a sheer delight to be with. He would scoot around on his backside, and, as he got older, we affectionately nicknamed him "Houdini," as he could escape from both his highchair and crib, even when strapped in place! Even the event of his birth was unusual—birthed right in the middle of the maternity wing hallway (another story for another time)!

Toby always seemed like a contemplative child, sucking his thumb and staring into a meaningful distant space. His epiphany was a welcome gift and reassurance that the Lord was at work among us, no matter what was happening around us.

Another great blessing at this time was making the acquaintance of a few faith-filled young Catholic married couples in the area. Above all, Jake and Tina Wagner became great family friends, sharing many wonderful times together: game nights, outings, church ministry, and collaborating with us to begin a pro-life pregnancy center named The Crossing of Manitowoc County, that is still in operation to this day by the grace of God.

Come Holy Spirit

As I approached the end of my master's in theological studies degree at Saint Norbert College, I began to explore new job possibilities. I really felt stymied at my 8-5 job, in which I pushed papers more than an expanding vision for ministry, and so I felt called to hunt for a new ministry position that would allow me to use my gifts more fully.

Over the Fourth of July weekend, 2006, Megan and our kids travelled to the Upper Peninsula of Michigan to visit family, while I stayed back home and composed my master's thesis of sixty pages, entitled, "The Good News of Jesus Christ," in only three days. I had done all of the preliminary research, had organized my ideas, and was ready to write. Sometime prior to this weekend, I remember driving home from class at Saint Norbert College one afternoon, right after I had determined to investigate the essence of the good news of Jesus by bringing together the theology of Joseph Ratzinger and Karl Rahner in harmonious confrontation. A jet black PT Cruiser passed me in the left lane of the highway with a license plate that read "BAD NUZ." In a strange way, this gave me even more confirmation about the project I was to complete, dedicated to the good news of Jesus.

My thesis centered around a wonderful verse in the Book of the Prophet Isaiah: "How beautiful upon the mountains are the feet of the one bringing good news, announcing peace, bearing good news, announcing salvation, saying to Zion, 'Your God is King!'" (52:7). I had ordered the critical edition of the Hebrew Scriptures, wanting to probe the original language in which this text and other related texts were written. I had taught myself to read Hebrew and Greek, first by learning the alphabets and then working with grammar books so that I could get the gist of the original biblical language texts. When my critical edition of the Hebrew Scriptures arrived, the book mysteriously was missing a section of pages that included chapter 52 of the Book of the Prophet Isaiah. This was further confirmation that I needed to press on with my intended project, so I had Amazon send me a new copy that included all the pages of the Hebrew Scriptures, including Isaiah 52.

Around the same time, I received an animated email from a representative of Holy Spirit Catholic Community in Naperville, Illinois, who was a member of their hiring committee for the director of youth ministry position. They wanted me to come there for an interview. I gladly went and had an awesome interview. It was a precarious and delicate ministry situation. The pastor had an allegation of sexual abuse against him, and, since it remained unsubstantiated, he continued to serve as pastor of the parish. I trusted in the mercy of God, not knowing many details about the situation, but I could tell that there was a highly trained and experienced staff there and I would fit in perfectly.

It was a good thing that I was offered the job soon thereafter because the pastor of Saint Peter the Fisherman had found out (to my surprise) that I had started to look for another job. He was not happy, to say the least! I accepted the new position at Holy Spirit Catholic Community with much thanksgiving, as I would be the director of the expansive youth ministry program there, reporting directly to the pastor. The pastor was a true servant-leader and a visionary. I suddenly was at home in a place I felt I could use my gifts to their maximum potential, getting paid over $25,000 more than my previous job.

Gone Fishing

Taking the reigns as director of youth ministry at Holy Spirit Catholic Community was an incredible change. I finally was properly credentialed as a lay minister in the church and I was plunged into a parish community that had hundreds of teens and extensive resources. The pastor trusted me, and he said so.

As with any ministry job, there were really high highs and really low lows. Fortunately, I would say that the highs completely outweighed the lows. The parish had wonderful facilities, including three large drop-down projector screens in the worship space and an intimate and prayerful Eucharist chapel. It was truly a postconciliar Catholic parish in which laity were empowered to lead and collaborate in ministry to the highest degree. I was thrilled to be in this place at this time.

The ministry that I witnessed and helped lead during my four years there was profoundly saturating. Lives of young people literally were saved. Countless conversion experiences were catalyzed. The church was alive as a home where young people found meaning, belonging, friendship, truth, love, and a God who called them by name. This was something I didn't exactly experience in my church growing up, so, looking back, I'm so glad it became a reality for the young people I served.

When I entered full-time ministry in the church in the year 2001, I cast my net out for a big catch (see Luke 5:1–11). My inherited last name, Wallenfang, means "whale catcher," after all! At Holy Spirit Catholic Community, I found myself fishing in deep waters with an abundance of people who, over time, found themselves caught in the net of divine grace. I loved to see the church full of teens who genuinely were attracted to the beauty, goodness and truth of the gospel of Jesus Christ and his merciful presence with them and in them.

My brother, Mike, Creagon and I with a successful catch of fish.

Over the course of four years, our youth ministry grew at least one-hundred-fold. A vibrant and charismatic woman had served as the director of youth ministry for several years before I arrived to take her place in leadership after she had moved on to a new field of ministry. I tried to continue those parts of the ministry that had been well-established, while building on them and tweaking them along the way. We went from around a dozen teens gathering together for Bible study, fellowship, and worship on a weekly basis to hundreds of teens and young adults participating and leading in ministry. One of the favorite songs we would sing was "Big House" by Audio Adrenaline. Talk about coming around full circle!

We ran three weekend-long high school retreats per year called DRY BONES, eventually witnessing over one-hundred teens voluntarily wanting to lead these retreats each year. Naperville was a hub for special education, and we began a ministry for young adults, KOINONIA, whose leadership included people with disabilities. This outreach ministry included weekly gatherings, occasional outings, and retreats. People with various disabilities served in leadership roles across our ministries, and dozens of adults were recruited to serve in ministry. We started a weekly large-group outreach to middle school students called THE EDGE, as well as a weekly outreach ministry to high school students called AFTERBURN. We hosted several Bible studies and sustained dozens of small discipleship groups every year. We had annual mission trips and many other social outings. I supervised three staff persons and two youth ministry interns and managed a budget of tens-of-thousands of dollars.

All in all, the youth ministry during those four years reached a zenith that I never could have imagined, but toward which I always had hoped. I was so thankful to be there and broke down in tears on many occasions, marveling at what the Lord was doing in our midst.

Scenes from a Steubenville High School Youth Conference, and a gathering of young adults for a Koinonia get-together in Naperville, Illinois.

Fire and Dove

New job, new house, new baby! On December 6, 2007, Callum Ignatius was born. Another beautiful boy! Megan and I liked unique names and names of saints. "Callum," of Irish origin, means "dove," and "Ignatius" means "fiery one." His name connected to the church at which I worked—Holy Spirit Catholic Community—as fire and dove are symbols of God the Holy Spirit.

Callum was baptized by full immersion, and I got to do the immersing while our pastor poured water over his head. For his baptism, Callum was clad in a red Fuzzy Bunz diaper, symbolic of the fire of the Holy Spirit. He had spent several days in the hospital after his birth because of high bilirubin levels, but, once we got passed that, it was so good to have him home.

At the time, we were renting a house on Chicago Avenue, near downtown Naperville. It was a lovely area and we were thriving, though trying not to get caught up in the materialism and vanity of the place. Hedonism is a natural tendency of human beings, and, when there's money to spend, pleasure tends to be sought after all the more.

That same year, I began to pursue something that I never thought I would: doctoral studies in theology. I loved to be at home with my family and I loved ministry. I had the perfect job and yet I felt that God was calling me to continue my studies, as they were one of the primary ways that I searched out his face. After all, I would find myself laying in our backyard hammock, reading Karl Rahner's *Foundations of Christian Faith* (not a Reader's Digest kind of book!) for the second time through.

Again, I was nothing stellar on paper to be qualified to apply to such a program. Nevertheless, I thought that I had a chance to get through the back door by taking classes, two at a time, and then perhaps being admitted to the program gradually. There really was only one option for Catholic doctoral studies in theology in the area: Loyola University Chicago, named after Saint Ignatius Loyola (another point of connection to Callum Ignatius's name!). I ended up taking the GRE in Sycamore, Illinois (reminiscent of Zacchaeus climbing the sycamore tree in the Gospel of Saint Luke), and enrolled in two classes for the winter 2007 semester: sexual ethics and the history of Christian theology. These were incredibly rigorous courses, but I held my own and was loving it.

I would go on to take two more courses in the fall (while still not officially in the program) and ended up being put on the waiting list for admission. It was such a difficult discernment process—almost a love-hate relationship. I enjoyed full-time ministry so much and I realized that completing a PhD in theology would result in a transition into full-time academia. I experienced not a few trials through my studies, and yet, through it all, I ultimately felt confirmed in this new layer of vocation. Megan was entirely supportive, and oftentimes it was she more than I who knew that I was called to this. In the end, I determined that, even if I was not admitted into Loyola's program, I would pursue other doctoral programs in theology, no matter if it required a move across the country.

Pictures of Megan, our children, and I.

The First Time's the Charm

As mentioned before, my Mom liked to say that I lived "a charmed life." It is true that I have often found this to be the case. In the eleventh hour, just when it seemed like my time had run out for getting into the PhD program in theology at Loyola University Chicago, I received a call from Dr. Robert DiVito, who was chair of the program at the time. He left me a voice message on my home phone, and they had a teaching assistantship offer for me!

Just like when I was offered my first full-time job, I leaped in the air with exaltation. I couldn't believe that this actually was happening. I had this magnet that I got from Loyola even before I was admitted that read: "When one 'L' door closes, another opens." This was with implicit reference to the Chicago "L" train that ran through campus. Here again it appeared that God had made a way out of no way. I was a nobody from nowhere and now found myself able to pursue a deep-seated passion to probe the truth with the greatest possible rigor.

A picture of the Loyola magnet that inspired me as I waited patiently for that door to open, while other doors would close.

Mama

Through the thick and thin of everything going on in my life, there was a quiet, faithful, and always interested cheerleader: my Mom, Linda. Since I had to commute an hour back and forth from Rogers Park (where we moved after I was admitted into Loyola) to Naperville, it was the perfect time to talk with my Mom on the ("hands-free") phone. I hardly can remember a time when I called, and she didn't answer. She was a constant in my life and I was a constant in hers.

We would talk about everything. I could tell hear about all my feelings, dreams, desires, successes, joys, failures and disappointments, and she loved to hear every word of it. She encouraged me without end and supported me every step of the way. Indeed, she noticed the little things and treasured them. And I would be an encouragement for her in her war of attrition against cancer.

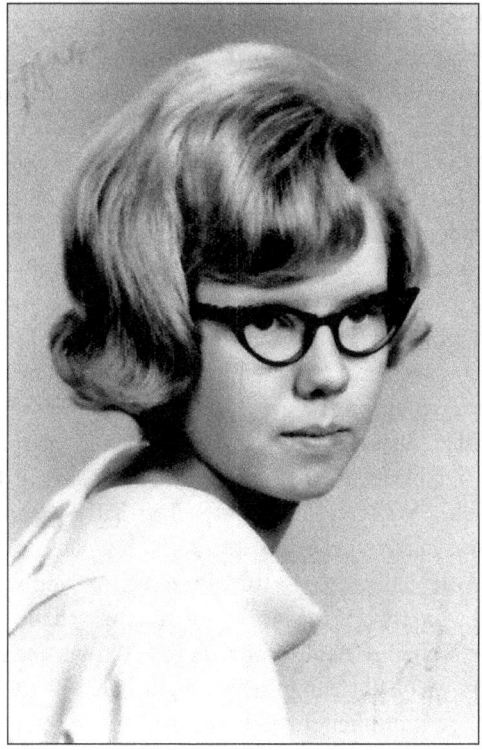

My mother, Linda Shultz, during her
junior year of high school.

Intensity

After being admitted into the program at Loyola, I took as many courses at a time as I could in order to finish the program as quickly as possible and transition into academia. I plunged into more coursework during the summer of 2008. One of the courses was called "Philosophy for Theologians," and it was taught by Dr. John McCarthy. It was a wonderful course and we explored the ancient Greeks through postmodernity.

One of the philosophers we studied was named Jean-Luc Marion. He was a phenomenologist. I had begun to learn about phenomenology during my time at Saint Norbert College, but the work of Marion intrigued me even more. I was studying these ideas at a whole new level. My affinity for Marion's work grew rapidly, and, the next thing I knew, our class took a "field trip" to the University of Chicago to attend one of Marion's public lectures. This particular lecture was entitled "Sketch of a Phenomenological Concept of Sacrifice."

As we walked toward the entrance of Swift Hall, the place where the lecture would be given, a man who clearly looked the part of a professor walked past me. He had on a sport coat, a bowtie, and looked pensively through thick glasses. I thought to myself, "Surely, this is a true scholar." I had heard that the University of Chicago was a type of "Ivy League" school of the Midwest. Sure enough, there was ivy climbing up and down its beautiful historic academic buildings.

This encounter with this unknown man left a deep impression on me. His face signified intensity and concentration. It was a serious look that was preoccupied with hidden abstract thoughts that were not distracted by all of the people passing by. Perhaps there was even a tinge of anxiety and stress upon this face that cut through the crowd. In any case, I was impressed by this visage that signaled the highest caliber of the academic enterprise.

We took our places in the lecture hall, and I sat in the back with some of my fellow students. It was a packed hall—eventually standing room only. It was hard to believe that so many people would come out by their own free will to hear this lecture. Professor Marion was introduced, and I was stunned. His was the face of the man who had walked past me outside, bowtie and all. He spoke English with a thick French accent and his presentation was bedazzling. I was caught hook, line, and sinker and pulled into the boat of phenomenology, and this presentation would set the course for my future life's work.

Camouflaged Street Poet

Yet I wasn't the only one preparing a life's work. A surprise encounter on the fringe of the campus of Loyola University Chicago would awaken appreciation of a world of depth I knew nothing about.

While going about my studies at Loyola, often on the run between work and home, I would frequent the Subway sandwich shop on the edge of campus. There were always homeless people milling about that area panhandling and looking for a place to belong. One day I met a poor man named Clark.

Clark asked me for any money I could spare, and I in turn asked him if he would like me to buy him lunch at Subway. He acquiesced and we ordered our sandwiches in the shop. After I paid for the food, Clark, taking his sandwich to go, asked me if he could share with me a poem. I said, "Sure."

While still in the restaurant, Clark delivered an exquisite yet dark and colorful poem about a woman who was forced into prostitution. As he performed his original composition, looking at me with penetrating bloodshot eyes, and christening me once again with his alcohol-laced breath and spittle, I could not help but be moved. I was not the sole benefactor that day, for Clark gave me a gift that surpassed my egocentric and self-congratulatory corporal work of mercy.

From Idol to Icon

While going about my studies at Loyola, I easily could be spotted across campus. I was the eccentric student who tended to tote at least one rolling suitcase behind me, if not two. I loved books, and I preferred to have them on hand, both for research and to reference during class discussions (my professors must have loved me!).

No matter where I was heading on campus, I always felt as if I was on a mission. The biblical verse that would pass through my mind frequently was Psalm 19:6. Speaking of how the sun proclaims the glory of God by "coming forth like a bridegroom from his canopy," it follows this image by describing the sun "like a champion joyfully runs his course." This is how I felt without fail at Loyola, pulling the suitcases of books behind me: "like a champion (who) joyfully runs his course."

I continued to be drawn to the works of Jean-Luc Marion. In several of his books, he distinguishes between the theological concepts of the idol and the icon. Through phenomenological description, he is able to tell the two apart and point to the power and authenticity of the icon for Christian belief and practice. An idol freezes the gaze of the onlooker, often merely reflecting the Narcissistic tendencies of the human heart. An icon, in contrast, is a personalistic portal that orients the self toward the other. A crossing of gazes transpires through the phenomenality of the icon and a world of persons, gift and love is opened. I found Marion's writings to be exceptionally compelling and I couldn't read enough of them.

As my coursework was nearing completion in the spring of 2009 (though I would take a slew of courses that semester), my overall credits and the course offerings were at variance just enough to give rise to a happily unexpected solution. I suddenly had the opportunity to take a course at the University of Chicago with Professor Marion and transfer the credit back to Loyola. But first, I had to be admitted to the Graham School there, and this procedure was not a given.

After my written application to the Graham School was accepted, I was called in for an interview with some of its staff people. I remember the morning well. I woke up feeling sick as can be, and I felt that it was virtually impossible for me to go in for the interview. Because I did not want to jeopardize my chance of being admitted, I somehow got myself ready and drove over to the U of C. I felt absolutely awful. The interview went well, nevertheless, and, soon thereafter, I discovered myself in the company of the Master, in Swift Hall, Room 106. It was a course on the phenomenological concept of givenness—the perfect fare for a budding phenomenologist.

The course was intense: reading the pioneering texts of Edmund Husserl, Martin Heidegger and others in their original German. I gained so much from the course and it actually turned out to be a rather mystical experience. I recall vividly the first class with Marion. I was eagerly awaiting his entrance into the classroom and suddenly he appeared with his customary serious visage while a young student seemed to be accompanying him, talking off his ear about some ancient Greek philosopher.

I frequented Professor Marion's office hours as much as possible, signing my name on his schedule at least once a week. These were delightful exchanges and I really had to pinch myself to be convinced that all this was really happening. However, I think my office visits may have become a bit excessive, because during one such visit, as I was working my way through a list of at least half-a-dozen questions I had prepared to ask him, he gently interrupted me and asked if I would excuse myself since he needed to work to prepare for his next class. This was a little disconcerting, and I proceeded to cross off my name of the schedule for future office hour meetings. I persevered in spite of this embarrassing incident and continued to have a cordial relationship with him.

Another incredibly divine experience for me was peeking my head into Bond Chapel, just behind Swift Hall, on several occasions after class. Whenever I would enter the chapel, there tended to be an Eastern Orthodox liturgy happening, replete with icons and incense. It was a rather surreal experience, and it sealed my purpose in taking class with Marion and absorbing his work. The campus of the University of Chicago is stunning in the springtime: so many flowering trees and old, stately buildings. I remember laying down on the lawn inside the quadrangle adjacent to Swift Hall, reading Heidegger. I was in my element. The place breathed of studiousness and this coincided with my personal mission.

On another occasion, I attended a public lecture sponsored by the Lumen Christi Institute. Marion was in attendance with his wife, Corinne. After the lecture, I was introducing myself to Corinne when he brought me a glass of wine. It was a memorable gesture of hospitality that I'll never forget, incarnating his phenomenology of gift and saturated phenomena.

Heart Mended

Immersed in doctoral-level studies, working a full-time job in youth ministry (always dealing with some kind of serious intervention), commuting two hours a day, raising four children and having a fifth one in womb, living in a big city and trying to make ends meet, the stress could tend to pile up subtly but surely.

One night I came home late from a youth ministry event, had drunk several caffeinated beverages, and ended up getting just a few hours of sleep. The next morning, I had gotten up to get ready, and, for a short while, I willingly succumbed to some fleeting lustful thoughts, even if perhaps to help alleviate the compounded stress that built up in my body and soul. I went to lay back down in bed and my heart began to palpitate in an unusual way.

This lasted over the next couple hours and I didn't know what was happening. I finally drove myself to the nearest emergency room and was attended to immediately. The doctors diagnosed me on the spot with atrial fibrillation. This sudden irregular condition of my heart, in which the electrical signals of the upper chambers become disorganized and uncoordinated in relation to the lower cambers, reflected the irregular, disorganized, uncoordinated and chaotic condition of my soul. Upon being wheeled through the emergency room on a gurney and down the hallway toward my designated room, I felt ashamed of my sins. I am a sinner, and, because of my sins, I had brought harm on myself and great risk to my family. Surely, I have not emphasized this fact enough in this book: I am a wretched sinner. Estranged from God and neighbor, alienated from self and other, I have failed often and miserably.

> The thought of my wretched homelessness is wormwood and poison; remembering it over and over, my soul is downcast. But this I will call to mind; therefore I will hope: The LORD's acts of mercy are not exhausted, his compassion is not spent; they are renewed each morning—great is your faithfulness! The LORD is my portion, I tell myself, therefore I will hope in him—For the Lord does not reject forever; though he brings grief, he takes pity, according to the abundance of his mercy; he does not willingly afflict or bring grief to human beings—What should the living complain about? About their sins! Let us search and examine our ways, and return to the LORD! Let us lift up our hearts as well as our hands toward God in heaven! We have rebelled and been obstinate—You drew near on the day I called you; you said, "Do not fear!" You pleaded my case, Lord, you redeemed my life (Lamentations 3:19-24, 31-33, 39-42, 57-58).

It is only because of the grace of God through Jesus Christ that I write this today. Great is his faithfulness and mercy—a mercy renewed even with the rising sun this morning! As a Catholic, I have frequented the sacraments of Eucharist and confession over the years. I owe it to these—to these channels of divine grace—that I have been healed and restored over and over and over again. I am not a perfect man, and I join with you in the solidarity of our imperfect past (see Psalm 14; Romans 3:23), as well as in the communal hope of our past, present and future redeemed.

I write this book, not as testimony of the glamour of sin, but as testimony to the delusiveness and destructiveness of sin and the happy trade for the glory of conversion and resurrection. If I really thought that various forms of vice were the gateway to happiness, I gladly would tell you so. But in my forty-plus years of life, I attest to the profligacy and emptiness of sinful ways of thinking, speaking and acting. This is the truth. There is nothing more certain. The proof is in the pudding. Consequences follow upon actions. We reap what we sow.

"If we say, 'We are without sin,' we deceive ourselves, and the truth is not in us. If we acknowledge our sins, he is faithful and just and will forgive our sins and cleanse us from every wrongdoing" (1 John 1:8-9). I have sinned. This is the truth. I am being redeemed by the mercy of God the Father and the gift of God the Holy Spirit offered through Christ Jesus, the eternal Son of God the Father. I am not being hyperbolic or overestimating my wrongdoing. I am not being too hard on myself. A transparent examination of conscience shows that there is something awry in my past. I need to be forgiven and reconciled with God and my neighbor. This is the essence of salvation and it is a gift that I cannot procure on my own, by my own power, arrived at by my own autonomous agency. I am needy—indeed, as one saint has put it, "a beggar before God."

I share with you this humiliating and scary incident in order to showcase the truth all the more. Again, this is not religious semantics. It is not a mere theological veneer, overlaying phenomena that can be reduced to natural causes explained away by the imperial empiricism of natural sciences. Rather, this is the thickness of reality that merits a humble self-indicting confession to come clean with what tends to be glossed over by the pretensions of a more "sophisticated" and self-exonerating worldview. My heart is in need of mending and I yield it over to the divine Heartmender to heal the rupture and make whole what has been fragmented and distended.

After being placed in the hospital room in which I would stay overnight, I drifted off to sleep, praying that this strange heart condition would resolve. I awoke a while later—almost from an innocuous prayerful torpor (a new *tardemah*, like Adam in Genesis 2 and like Abraham in Genesis 15)—with gratitude and tears upon finding that my heart had resumed its restful sinus rhythm. I was grateful to God and this experience was serving as a wake-up call in a lot of ways.

Megan and my kids came to visit me the next morning in the hospital room. My kids had drawn me pictures of hope and love. One was an image of a heart—indeed, a heart mended.

Our Lady of the Wayside

So often at Loyola, when I would be lugging my rolling suitcases full of books behind me, I would walk past the front of the Madonna Della Strada Chapel. Its Italian name means "Our Lady of the Wayside." This image calls to mind Psalm 110:7: "He shall drink from the stream by the wayside and therefore he shall lift up his head." Just as Jesus was refreshed by the victorious "wayside" of his mother, so was I. I depended on her intercession constantly.

The "Hail Mary" prayer was inscribed in Latin over the front door of the chapel. I came to memorize this Latin version of the prayer by heart because I would walk past it so frequently.

> Ave Maria, gratia plena, Dominus tecum. Benedicta tu in mulieribus et benedictus fructus ventris tui, Iesus. Sancta Maria,

Mater Dei, ora pro nobis peccatoribus nunc et in hora mortis nostrae. Amen.

I had many reasons to duck into this chapel to pray. So many needs of so many people cried out for prayerful intervention. Within this chapel, I was inspired by the stained-glass windows of the saints—especially those of Our Blessed Mother, Saint Joseph, Saint Ignatius of Loyola, Saint Francis Xavier, Saint Thomas Aquinas, and Saint Thomas More. I felt that I was meant to be at this place to study and to pray. I loved the Jesuit values and tradition, feeling at home in an atmosphere of studiousness and the richness of the Catholic heritage.

Later in 2009 came a pastor change at Holy Spirit Catholic Community. I was hoping for the best with the transition, but it was not meant to be. Within a matter of months, I began to notice "the writing on the wall": this would be my final year working there as it was becoming apparent that my annual contract would not be renewed. Within the first year and a half of this new pastor's assignment, virtually all of the highly trained and experienced staff members would be let go. With little to no checks and balances of clerical power in the parish setting, pastors can tend to get away with that sort of thing.

It was a difficult final year for me at the parish, to say the least. Yet, "when one 'L' door closes, another opens." A biblical text that reassured me through all that was going on was Romans 8:28: "All things work together for good for those who love God and are called according to his purpose." It is quite scary to be laid off from a job being married, with five children to feed and raise. I would fall to my knees in the Madonna Della Strada Chapel and trust that the Lord would see us through these uncontrollable challenges and changes.

Sign of Peace

"New house, new job, new baby!" Once again, in the middle of a surging storm of life's uncertainties, a great certainty was born into the light of day. His name was Simeon Irenaeus, meaning "sign of peace." Just before we moved away from Chicago, Simeon was born on May 20, 2010. What another bundle of joy to delight our family!

From the start, Simeon showed himself to be an inquisitive child—always attentive and wanting to be held facing out to take in the world. In the thick of the shadows of life, God supplied a sign of peace that would allow Megan and I to trust in his providential care and the new land he was yet to show us. Like Abraham and Sarah, we would have to march through the darkness of faith in order to arrive on the other side of the promise. This is a very strenuous thing to do—to go about living at the hand of the Lord when you wish you just could live at the provision of your own. "The eyes of all who look hopefully to you; you give them their food in due season. You open wide your hand and satisfy the desire of every living thing" (Psalm 145:15–16).

Dark Nights

My Mom offered for my family and I to stay at her home for the next year while I wrote my dissertation and tried to find a full-time faculty position. We lived out of her basement. I would wake up very early in the morning and work on the dissertation for eight hours straight every day. Similar to how I wrote my master's thesis in three days, I wrote (a much longer) doctoral dissertation in three months. I was told that I completed the doctoral studies in theology program at Loyola faster than any other student in its history—and all this while working full-time, commuting two hours a day, having more babies, getting laid off, and being a complete underdog kind of a student. Only by the grace of God.

This year of working so hard, yet being "unemployed," was the most trying year of my life. I suffered a great deal mentally due to the mounting anxiety about finding a new full-time job, all the while collecting unemployment money. I applied for dozens and dozens of faculty positions around the country, but it wouldn't be until after I defended my dissertation in February of 2011 that I would get serious looks from universities. It was a highly competitive field and finding a faculty position was anything but guaranteed.

The psychological anguish at times was intense and terrifying. Fortunately, it wouldn't last long, but it's amazing how much a man in my shoes depends on full-time gainful employment. I felt as if I were in a kind of holding pen until landing a new job. It really felt like a year of humiliation and impossible patience. It all felt like a suffocating dark night of the soul.

CHAPTER 7

RENDEZVOUS WITH DESTINY

Emmanuel

IN THE MEANTIME, I was enjoying doing research on my dissertation topic: a phenomenology of the Eucharist. I was using the method of phenomenology to discover the meaning and truth of the Eucharist. One philosopher I was beginning to read a lot was Emmanuel Levinas. I had heard about him in passing several times during my studies at Loyola, but never got a chance to read his books until toward the end of my coursework there and then during the time I composed my dissertation.

The writings of Levinas had influenced Marion's work significantly. Like Marion, Levinas focused attention away from the self and instead on the other. But the difference was that Marion's other was the gift in general, while Levinas's other was the face of the other human within an ethical relationship. Levinas positioned ethics as "first philosophy." As a Jewish man whose parents, siblings and many other family members and friends were murdered in the Holocaust, Levinas understood the anthropological necessity of prioritizing ethics in philosophy.

Levinas shows how it is inappropriate and irresponsible to try to reduce the other to the same. In the face of the other is an otherness I cannot reduce, but for whom I am to become responsible. I was so impressed with the work of Levinas, and it ended up featuring prominently in my dissertation as a counterpart to that of Marion. Even more, the work of Levinas was influencing how I was living and reinforcing the fact that the world did not revolve around me. I was not at the center of the universe after all—but happily so.

A Stranger in a Strange Land

In my attempt to land a full-time faculty position in theology, I worked tirelessly to rack up as many academic conference presentations and publications as I could muster. Between the years 2009–2011, I would make no less than twenty-two presentations, from Chicago, to New York, to Phoenix, to Atlanta, to Nairobi, Kenya!

My trip to Nairobi was wonderful and terrifying at the same time. I traveled alone, bringing a message to share about Marion's phenomenology of givenness as applied to human personhood. I remember falling asleep in the plane, somewhere over the expanse of the Atlantic Ocean. I woke up with the feeling of slight anxiety that I was flying thousands of feet above the Atlantic, heading toward a land where I knew no one and no one knew me.

Upon arriving at the airport in Nairobi, I was to be picked up by a driver and transported to a Franciscan monastery on the outskirts of the Catholic University of Eastern Africa. The drive was fast and furious. When we arrived at the monastery, there was a guard with guard dogs. My bedroom window had metal bars outside, and there was a mosquito net tied up above my bed (that I did not realize I should have used until the next morning!). A thought that kept on coming to mind, to quote from *The Wizard of Oz*, was, "We're not in Kansas anymore, Toto!"

The first morning I awoke covered in mosquito bites and I had not gotten a malaria vaccination prior to my departure from the United States. Fortunately, I was able to take some medicine at the campus health clinic (though I had a terrible allergic reaction to the medicine once returning to Chicago).

As it turned out, the papal nuncio of Kenya at the time, Archbishop Alain Paul Lebeaupin, made a few opening remarks at the start of the conference and remained in the audience for my presentation. It was a quite sensational experience! Overall, my trip to Nairobi was very eye-opening and soul-transforming. I came to realize just a little more how big, beautiful and diverse the world really is.

Train Station

The year that Megan, our kids and I lived with my Mom was completely gifted. Being able to spend so much time with my Mom while she was undergoing chemotherapy was fortunate. Even though it seemed like a great setback to have to live with my Mom at thirty-two years of age, it was beneficial for her and Megan, our kids and me. Often, it's not until you are living without grandparents that you realize how much they mean to you. So, I was thankful that my own children had a chance to live with Grandma for a year and get to know her so well.

That year my Mom would get up early in the morning on some days to drop me off at two different train stations so that I could go into Chicago for student teaching. Sometimes she would drop me off at the South Shore Line stop in Michigan City, Indiana, and other times at the Amtrak stop below the bluff in Saint Joseph to catch the Pere Marquette Line. I treasured those car rides and waiting for the train with my Mom. It felt so right to be that "champion who runs his course" with his Mom so proud of him. I had come such a long way and now was nearing the end of my doctoral degree, and my Mom knew all the details of my history.

Waiting for the train and riding on the train were very spiritual and symbolic experiences. In them were the feelings of anticipation, patience, excitement, surprise, wonder, purpose, mission and destination. For both my Mom and I, the train signified life and our ultimate destination in heaven. Her husband (my father) had preceded us there, and now we were waiting for that eschatological train to pick us up and take us home.

Piece of Cake

The day for my dissertation defense had arrived. It was March of 2011. Marion was a member of my dissertation committee. My Mom, Jim and Cynda Muldoon, and several of my fellow graduate students would be in attendance on the campus of Loyola University Chicago. How was Professor Marion going to travel from the University of Chicago on the south side of the city to the north side where Loyola was located? I was to pick him up!

When you first meet Professor Marion, he is all business. When you go to pick him up to travel to your dissertation defense, he is even more so. Coming to his office to collect him, he donned his long tweed coat over his shoulders like a superhero's cape and walked at a quickened pace down the stairs of Swift Hall and out of the building. He was walking in front of me, though he did not even know where the car was parked!

Finally, we made it to the car, and I began to drive. I tried to make small talk and the Professor seemed rather tight-lipped. We passed the Museum of Science and Industry. I remember going there on several occasions as a child. I asked Professor Marion if he had ever been there before, and, without hesitation, in a stern voice, he said, "I was there before you were born!" There was no question who really was in the driver's seat on that morning!

We entered the building for my defense—the same building that housed the Subway sandwich shop that I would frequent throughout the course of my studies there. I remember observing the way Marion would gaze at things. Very carefully, absorbantly and inquisitively. I could see his phenomenological approach at work in how he perceived and received the world. He had a playful side in there somewhere and it was fun to see that come out a little bit. He asked for coffee and I got him some.

The defense went very well. Everyone was asked to step out of the room at its conclusion, while a verdict was made by the committee in private. Then we all were invited back in. And the verdict? "Passed with distinction!" This was the highest rating for the dissertation defense and I already had achieved this rating on my comprehensive exams. I was elated and so was everyone else in the room, including my Mom.

The next thing I knew, as friends were expressing their congratulations to me, was that Professor Marion presented me with a piece of cake. Reminiscent of when he brought me the glass of wine at the Lumen Christi presentation, the piece of cake signified the gift. It signified God's grace—a gift of which I was not worthy, but was coming in my direction anyway.

After dropping off Marion back at the University of Chicago (the conversation on the way back went much better than the conversation on the way to the defense!), I drove home to Saint Joseph. Before going to the house to tell Megan all about the defense, I stopped by the perpetual Eucharistic adoration chapel at Saint Joseph Catholic Church—the place of my first full-time job. I entered the chapel and fell to my knees in great thanksgiving. It was such a special day and I had to give credit where credit was due. A full-circle moment indeed, and I basked in the goodness of the Lord.

Sometime later I would have a dream in which I saw Professor Marion at the front of the classroom teaching. Mysterious writing appeared on his face—it looked like Chinese, or some kind of east Asian script. I did not know exactly the meaning of this dream for me, as it seemed to point to some future fulfillment. Yet, one thing I knew for sure, was that he had more to teach me.

Checkmate

Right before moving in with my Mom, I had received the news that one of my long-time friends, Sathish (Andrea) Sundaram, had suffered an accident. He was going horse-riding with one of his friends, and, upon mounting his horse, fell off and hit his head on a fence. He immediately became paralyzed from the neck down.

Before this accident, Sathish had gone to Harvard University and completed a bachelor's degree in physics. He then had gone to the University of Toronto and earned a master's degree in Italian literature. He was a cosmopolitan man—travelling the world, playing multiple instruments, and enjoying the good things afforded by so many beautiful and diverse cultures around the world.

Right before the accident, he was employed full-time as an engineer at Whirlpool in Saint Joseph, Michigan. Even though he had macular degeneration in his eyes and so couldn't drive and hardly could see, he lived in a house on his own and was doing quite well. Following the accident, Sathish moved back in with his parents in Saint Joseph, where they would be able to care for him.

Since I was living with my Mom that year, just down the road, I was able to visit with Sathish every week. He is an audiophile, so we often would listen to music together, have deep conversation, and play chess. Since he could not move his arms and hands, I would move his pieces for him. It was a glorious time and I witnessed the depths of love and determination in he and his parents that year. Sathish, a name that means "married to the Lord of truth," taught me much about the power of truth as it reveals itself to us in this life.

The following fall, Sathish and his parents would move to Pittsburgh, PA, so that he could attend the University of Pittsburgh doctoral program in rehabilitation engineering. I had encouraged him to pursue further studies, and I was thrilled that he was taking the risk to do something he loved, even though it meant a big move for he and his parents. He is flourishing there to this day and we still will get together for dinner and concerts once in a while. We also have been known to keep up our chess competitions online, and Sathish tends to be victorious.

Sathish, my parents and I.

Rendezvous with Destiny—Part I

As mentioned earlier, in preparation for landing a university faculty position, I worked hard to build up my Curriculum Vitae. I presented at numerous conferences, even all the way to Nairobi, Kenya. In February of 2011, I was scheduled to present a paper at the Edith Stein Project conference at the University of Notre Dame. The name of the paper was "Awaken, O Spirit: The Vocation of Becoming in the Work of Edith Stein."

I had begun to study the life and writings of Edith Stein toward the end of my time at Loyola as well. Ever since I first encountered her life back in my middle school days while exploring the lives of saints, I was intrigued. She was raised in a Jewish family, became atheist, earned a doctorate in philosophy studying with Edmund Husserl, was baptized as a Catholic at the age of thirty, became a Discalced Carmelite nun, and finally would be deported to Auschwitz to be executed in a gas chamber on August 9, 1942. She was a martyr to truth, and I wanted to follow her in the way she thought and lived toward truth.

At this conference, I was able to meet one of the preeminent theology professors at Notre Dame: Dr. John Cavadini. He gave a keynote presentation on the universal call to holiness. At the end of his presentation, during the Q&A time, I asked him a question related to chapter 11 on time in Saint Augustine's *Confessions*. I knew he was an Augustine scholar, and he seemed to appreciate my question.

Following his presentation, I came up to him to introduce myself. He was sitting next to his wife, Nancy. I happened to have a copy of my dissertation on hand and showed it to him. He seemed very interested and impressed with the project. I told him that I was on the hunt for a faculty position and he said that Holy Cross College, across the street from Notre Dame, had an opening for its chair in theology. We continued to get to know each other over the course of the conference, and, by the end, he said that he would support my candidacy for that position.

Annunciation

Following the Edith Stein conference, I was in correspondence with Holy Cross College, as well as a few other schools who seemed interested in me. One afternoon, Megan, our kids and I swung by the grocery store. She ran in to get a few things while I stayed in the car with our kids. I began to pray the Rosary with them. Just when I announced the first Joyful Mystery, "The Annunciation," my cell phone rang. It was Fr. Patrick Manning from Walsh University in North Canton, Ohio. They wanted me to come to campus for an interview! I said yes without hesitation.

Soon thereafter, I got another invitation for an on-campus interview at Divine Word College in Epworth, Iowa, a seminary for Catholic missionaries. On the second day of that interview, I got a voice message from the provost at Walsh University. He wanted me to call him back. On the same day, I got a call from Holy Cross College, wanting me to come for an on-campus interview as well.

The interview went brilliantly at Divine Word College, but they had one more candidate to interview, so they were not able to offer me the job just yet. As I was driving home in the rental car through the rolling hills of Iowa country, I called back the provost at Walsh University. He offered me the job! After I got off the phone, I was crying tears of joy and victory. The dark days of unemployment were coming to a close and a new chapter of life was about to begin. Ave Maria, gratia plena . . .

Amish Country

When my family and I came to search for a house to buy in Ohio, we stayed with our new friends, the Gerbers. Dr. Chad Gerber was a theology professor at Walsh, and we hit it off right away. Our families had a lot in common and they welcomed us with open arms and hearts as we ventured out in this new territory of work and life.

Chad introduced me to the beautiful lands of Wayne and Holmes counties—home to the largest Amish community in the United States. I remember the first time he and I drove up to the top of a tall hill overlooking the picturesque rolling fields and autumn leaves near the home in which he was raised. It was a breathtaking view, and Chad, his wife, Jen, and family eventually would build their own home on that very land. Friendship and fraternity are among the Lord's greatest gifts to us, and there are some friendships that never fade, but linger into eternity. This was one of them.

Can I Get a Witness?

Upon moving to Canton, Ohio, home of the Professional Football Hall of Fame, I felt like there was something very fitting about being there. Yet it was no longer being inducted into the Professional Football Hall of Fame that I was interested in. Instead, I now was interested in being inducted into a different Hall of Fame, or, perhaps better put, Hall of Humility: The Communion of Saints.

Our family settled in the area and I immediately became involved in the local pro-life movement, not so much as a political lobbying group as simply a witness to the totality of life, advocating for those persons who could not speak for themselves. I met a wonderful man who was a leader in the local pro-life movement, Pastor Walter Moss. He was African American and a strong defender of life. We got together for breakfast and began to collaborate in witnessing to the truth, goodness and beauty of life. I invited him to speak in some of my classes at Walsh University, and he invited me to speak at his church and at another African American church. I also spoke at local pro-life meetings. I had a story to share, and the title of my talk was "Amnesia." Here it is in full:

The title of my talk is "Amnesia" and has everything to do with forgetting and not forgetting.

We gather in thanksgiving for the 40 Days for Life Vigil. By visibly keeping watch ourselves, we cause others to awake from their slumber and complacency. We cause others to "think again" and recognize that there is something dreadfully amiss in our culture today. By visibly keeping watch, we cause passersby to question such a serious and unwavering statement of non-violent, prayerful resistance. We thank God for the demonstration and message of 40 Days for Life and pray that it may serve as a symbol of our daily struggle for justice for all people, no matter how big, small or able. For together we are able.

I would like to begin by telling the story of a person who, because others refused to forget him, was given the gift of life, time and time again.

There was an infant who was conceived out of wedlock. As the story goes, his natural father was married and had several children, but his natural mother was not married and had no children of her own. Yet this infant child nevertheless was conceived within her through an adulterous relationship. The place was Kalamazoo, Michigan. The year was 1977 and the response of the mother to the life of her newly conceived child hung in the balance. In a post-Row v. Wade nation, no infant is automatically granted security, not even in his or her own mother's womb.

In such a precarious predicament, this mother could have willed the termination of her little child's life, without penalty and without delay, and then seemingly gone on her merry way. She could have chosen to reject the silent yet acute call of her child to care for him; she could have resisted his will to live within her and through her. She was alone, yet not alone. Her and him, the him within. Tossing and turning—what is a mother to do—a mother who in despair does not feel that she can raise this child in a loving and nurturing environment? She is not ready. She lacks a support structure. She lacks the resources. She lacks.

In spite of all this, with greatest courage and strength, hoping against all hope, she contacted an adoption agency and resolved to bring her child to term. This she does, and on February 24, 1978, she gives birth to a beautiful baby boy. His hair burns fire-red and the voice of gratitude is heard in his cries as he gasps for his first breaths of air and is placed in her compassionate arms. Soon thereafter, the mother lets go. She gives him up, not to die, but to go on living in a home of love and welcome. She requests that he be placed in a Christian family who loves academics, music and sports. She has selflessly run her race with her son and passes off the torch of life to him and his new family, for him to continue this race of perseverance and the will to live.

The child goes on to stay with a foster family until he is assigned a permanent family in which to intermingle his life with theirs. His new adoptive parents reside in the city of Benton Harbor, Michigan. They love academics, music and sports. The father is a college professor of political science, and the mother works at a newly formed art and framing business. These parents were unable to have children naturally, so they decided to adopt this baby boy as their own. Benton Harbor is a diverse and ethnically rich community, with 90% of its population being African-American. Across the river is the city of Saint Joseph, with 90% of its population being European-American. Needless to say, this demographic dynamic made for an ambivalent locale in which this child was to grow up and receive his formative education.

The child attends a parochial school from kindergarten until the twelfth grade. He was then awarded a Presidential scholarship to study pre-medicine and play football at Albion College. During his time there, he became more interested in music, even singing in a Black Gospel choir with his college roommates and other friends. He eventually graduated with a bachelor's degree in trumpet performance. In May of 2000, he was married and he and his wife's first child was born on April 30, 2001, a baby girl named Ellen Agnes. Five more children were conceived by and born of this couple over the years to follow. The father ended up going into full-time youth ministry for a decade and eventually earned his master's and Ph.D. degrees in Theology, that is, "the study of God."

The God who he continues to study and to love deeply is the one who brings him here tonight to share a few fragments of his story with the hope of testifying to the power of life and love. For such testimony perhaps brings us to the threshold of the meaning of life: to love as God loves. To become a total gift of oneself in order to breathe life into another. Is this not for what we have been created? Is this not the courageous course set before us, calling us onward to victory—a victory not only our own, but a victory shared by all?

It is with this victory in mind that I make my own the words of the prophet, Jeremiah:

> "There is in my heart as it were a burning fire
> shut up in my bones,
> and I am weary with holding it in,
> and I cannot."

Or again, as Job's friend Elihu exclaims:

> "Behold, my heart is like wine that has no vent;
> like new wineskins, it is ready to burst.
> I must speak, that I may find relief;
> I must open my lips and answer."

Together we remember once more that there is nothing short of genocide occurring throughout our land today. Totaling millions upon millions of human beings go on being executed on a daily basis throughout our country and throughout the world. This statement is no political ploy or exaggerated rhetoric. This is simply stating the truth—a truth at which all human beings of goodwill and sound reason should be outraged.

When we as a nation have lost our wits to the point of regarding the status of the personhood of the infant as up-for-grabs, to be arbitrarily decided by a handful of so-called "Justices"; when we as a nation have found it necessary to mandate ideologically-charged sex education classes in public schools that claim to be morally neutral but in fact poison the truth and meaning of human sexuality, namely, the truth of becoming a sincere gift of self to another in the permanent bond of marriage; when we as a nation have turned human life into a commodity, manufacturing human beings in the laboratory to be manipulated and destroyed in the name of an alleged good cause; when we as a nation replace self-control with birth control, thereby undermining the dignity of our sexuality and the gift of the child—we have effectively forgotten what it is to love as God loves, to be our brother's, our sister's, keeper.

The convicting words of the prophet, Isaiah, must sadly be proclaimed again in our day:

> "Woe to those who call evil good
> and good evil,
> who put darkness for light
> and light for darkness,
> who put bitter for sweet
> and sweet for bitter!
> Woe to those who are wise in their own eyes,
> and shrewd in their own sight!"

Instead of assuming responsibility for the most vulnerable persons among us, many persons in power dodge responsibility to their own, and to their children's, destruction. In the name of selfish rights and a myopic understanding of human freedom, certain members of our society have chosen to masquerade as messengers of light, when in fact devoid of humanizing enlightenment.

As French philosopher, Blaise Pascal, insightfully wrote almost 400 years ago:

> "This is my place in the sun. That is how the usurpation of the whole world began."

Pascal recognized that human beings assault the basic rights and liberties of one another by exercising personal power in an egotistical and self-interested fashion. To first of all and finally be concerned with staking out one's own "place in the sun" is to neglect to make room for one's neighbor; it is to essentially forget one's neighbor:

This is Adam and Eve wanting to be like God but forgetting who God really was.

This is the People of Israel asking Samuel for a human king to rule over them even though the one true God was their rightful and eternal King.

This is the crowd demanding Barabbas while condemning Jesus to a death he did not deserve.

As it turns out, our culture must urgently consider the claim of Spiderman's uncle Ben:

> "With great power comes great responsibility."

Instead, many people regard great power as license to define, manipulate and suppress the dignity and rights of others, especially the most vulnerable others among us. Many people believe that with more power comes less responsibility. Many people have sold out to a contraceptive mentality in a fast food culture, living instead by the well-known Burger King slogan, "your way right away." People have come to believe that the true meaning of freedom is to do what you want when you want with nothing getting in your way.

Nevertheless, the call remains the same: "With great power comes great responsibility." My favorite writer is twentieth-century Jewish French philosopher, Emmanuel Levinas. Levinas writes that "the human is the being who recognizes saintliness as the forgetting of self." In other words, to live as a saint is to forget oneself for the sake of the other. Because of the constant call to become responsible for the other, I am happily confronted with the possibility of forgetting myself by becoming a total gift of myself to the other who beckons me. Further, Levinas writes, "the more I am just the more I am responsible; one is never quits with regard to the other." Again, in other words, justice is a matter of becoming responsible for the other. To be just is to assume responsibility for the other. More precisely, to be just is to respond affirmatively to the presence of the other, the needs of the other—above all, to love and care for the other—not to forget the other. To remember the other is to be responsible for the other.

According to Levinas, who wrote his philosophy in response to the horrors of the Jewish Holocaust during World War II, the number one tragedy of humanity is forgetfulness of the other. The solution, then, to undo this tragic forgetfulness of the other is to forget oneself for the sake of the other. Amnesia of the needs of the other is cancelled out by a self-amnesia of love. This is to become a total and sincere gift of self, holding nothing back—a self-giving to the point of abandonment. As it turns out, this is the logic of the cross, the law of love—a gift which is received to the measure that it is given away.

We recall the words of the Rev. Dr. Martin Luther King in his 1963 letter from the Birmingham jail: "Injustice anywhere is a threat to justice everywhere," and further, "justice too long delayed is justice denied." Not only is there injustice here and there in the United States today, there is injustice everywhere. When infants are being mass-murdered all around us, and when organizations like Planned Parenthood claim to be doing women a favor by seeing to it that their own children are put to death, injustice reigns and liberty is denied. To quote again from Dr. King, "We know through painful experience that freedom is never voluntarily given by the oppressor; it must be demanded by the oppressed." But what if the oppressed have no voice with which to demand their own freedom and most fundamental right to life? Someone must take up their cause on their behalf; someone must make the plight of the infant their own. For the word "infant" means "one without a voice." Yet we can hear the infant calling out loudly through the form of his or her real and undeniable presence: "Care for me and love me!" We hear the voice of the infant through our own affirmative response to their silent yet acute call to recognize their personhood and intrinsic right to life. "With great power comes great responsibility."

As Nelson Mandela has said:

> "Our deepest fear is not that we are inadequate.
>> Our deepest fear is that we are powerful beyond measure.
>> It is our light, not our darkness that most frightens us.
>> You are a child of God. Your playing small doesn't serve the world.
>> There is nothing enlightened about shrinking so that other people
>> won't feel insecure around you.

We are all meant to shine.

As we let our light shine, we unconsciously give other people permission

to do the same.

As we are liberated from our own fear, our presence automatically

liberates others."

"We are all meant to shine," and, to quote Dr. King once more, we are not merely to be "a thermometer that records the ideas and principles of popular opinion" but are to be "the thermostat that transforms the mores of society." We find ourselves in the midst of a new chapter in the civil rights movement. When freedom and justice are being denied the most vulnerable persons among us, all human freedom and justice are thereby undermined. Some may argue, "But it is legal to terminate the life of the infant in the womb," to which I would reply with the words of Saint Augustine, "An unjust law is no law at all." Many people in power have forgotten the timeless wisdom of an elephant named Horton: "A person's a person no matter how small."

What we need to do as we go forth from this sacred place tonight is to continue to cultivate what the late Joseph Cardinal Bernardin called "a consistent ethic of life" which manifests itself as a seamless garment of life begetting life. Such a constant ethic devoted to life affirmatively responds to the call of the other in all situations and circumstances: coming to the assistance of the man who has no job, coming to the assistance of the woman with child who has been abandoned by family and friends, coming to the assistance of the elderly person in the nursing home who has no one to visit her, coming to the assistance of the child who needs help learning how to read, coming to the assistance of the person who has tested positive for HIV and has become ostracized, coming to the assistance of one's allies and enemies alike. For a "consistent ethic of life" is not selective in who it chooses to love and serve. A "consistent ethic of life" is devoted to all without exception, for God "makes his sun rise on the evil and the good, and sends rain on the just and the unjust." To show partiality is to neglect the demands of the "consistent ethic of life." In short, the "consistent ethic of life" refuses to forget the vocation to life and love of all God's children.

In closing, when the fourteenth chapter of Exodus says, "the LORD will fight for you, and you have only to be still," this does not mean that God is going to turn the tide of the cancerous "culture of death" overnight while we sit around and wait. Rather, as Saint Paul exhorts Saint Timothy, "preach the word, be urgent in season and out of season, convince, rebuke, and exhort, be unfailing in patience and in teaching—always be steady, endure suffering, do the work of an evangelist, fulfil your ministry." May we never cease to be instruments of God's mercy and justice in season and out of season; may we together be champions for life, breathing life into all people without hope; and may we never forget that "with great power comes great responsibility" by forgetting ourselves for the sake of our neighbors, living constantly to become our brother's, our sister's, keeper and friend.

"Lift Every Voice and Sing" by *James Weldon Johnson*

Lift every voice and sing, till earth and heaven ring
Ring with the harmonies of liberty;
Let our rejoicing rise, high as the list'ning skies,
Let it resound loud as the rolling sea.
Sing a song full of the faith
that the dark past has taught us,
Sing a song full of the hope
that the present has brought us;
Facing the rising sun of our new day begun,
Let us march on till victory is won.

Stony the road we trod, bitter the chast'ning rod,
Felt in the days when hope unborn had died;
Yet with a steady beat, have not our weary feet,
Come to the place for which our fathers sighed?
We have come over a way
that with tears has been watered.
We have come, treading our path
thro' the blood of the slaughtered,
Out from a gloomy past, till now we stand at last
Where the white gleam
of our bright star is cast.

God of our weary years, God of our silent tears,
Thou who has brought us thus far on the way;
Thou who hast by thy might, led us into the light,
Keep us forever in the path, we pray.
Lest our feet stray from the places

Our God where we met Thee,
Lest our hearts drunk with the wine of the world
we forget Thee;
Shadowed beneath Thy hand
May we forever stand,
True to our God,
True to our native land.

My children along the shore of the James River at the original Jamestown settlement in Virginia.

Hooker

Soon after we moved to Ohio, I was called to jury duty at the local courthouse. This was the first time in my life that I was summoned to jury duty. As for most people, I begrudgingly went, as this civic responsibility interrupted my week. The jury selection process commenced at the courthouse, "*voir dire*," and I was chosen as one of the dozen jurors to sit for the trial.

The case involved a woman who was arrested for prostitution. I couldn't believe it. Here I was, a man with a lustful heart, to sit as judge and juror of a woman who was the victim of mine and other men's lusts? It was she who should have been sitting in judgment of me!

The trial proceeded and there was ample evidence that she was guilty of prostitution. The time came for the jurors to go into the back room to decide the case. I was chosen by my fellow jurors to serve as the foreman for the case. After accepting the role, I said to the rest of the jury that it was important to remember that this woman was on trial due to the lusts of men.

Nevertheless, we had to do due diligence and come to a verdict as to whether or not there was sufficient evidence, beyond a shadow of a doubt, that this woman committed the act of prostitution. We arrived at the consensus that there was sufficient evidence and she was sentenced to thirty days in prison as punishment for her crime, yet it was I who felt as guilty as sin.

After the trial, I looked into bailing her out of jail. There was no bail set on her release from prison. All I could do was to pray for her and to continue to ask for forgiveness for my own sins.

Shoeless

Over the course of my life, I became attracted to the Carmelite saints. I already mentioned Saint Edith Stein (Teresa Benedicta of the Cross) above. Also, there were Saints Teresa of Ávila, John of the Cross, Thérèse of Lisieux, Elizabeth of the Trinity and many more. In Canton, I was in the process of writing a book on the work of Saint Edith Stein and reading through the collected works of Saint John of the Cross. Pope Saint John Paul II was influenced greatly by Carmelite spirituality, and this influence shined forth in his work called the *Theology of the Body*. I was teaching this work in full, as well as Saint Teresa of Ávila's *Interior Castle* and Saint Thérèse of Lisieux's *Story of a Soul*.

One day, Megan suggested that we look to find out if there was a Third Order Carmelite group in the area. There was, and we were welcomed with open arms. Megan and I both became Secular Discalced Carmelites, and it was a six-year process to make definitive promises. The name Megan chose was Veronica of Christ the Bridegroom, and the name I chose was Emmanuel Mary of the Cross.

This was a life-giving community and greatly strengthened our walk with the Lord. It will be left to another book to tell the story of our evolution as Secular Discalced Carmelites. Suffice it to say that "discalced" means "shoeless," and we loved approaching life, along with our children, in a barefoot kind of way.

Midnight Departure

One of the highlights during my time at Walsh University was hosting Jean-Luc Marion as the keynote speaker for our annual Philosophy-Theology Symposium. He came to talk about the phenomenology of the gift, and I could not have been more thrilled. I got to teach a seminar that semester entitled "Erotic Phenomena and Divinity." The catch was that I had to go pick up Marion by car in Chicago and bring him to North Canton, Ohio. Reminiscent of the morning of my dissertation defense, I was happy to serve as chauffeur, however, since it would afford hours of conversation together. I'm not sure he was as thrilled as me!

Professor Marion and I ended up having a wonderful time on the road together. We had amazing conversation about philosophy, theology and life. He was one of my great mentors—even heroes. I had the deepest admiration for his work, as it helped me to have faith in the fullness of God's revelation in Christ, supported by the most rational and relevant underpinnings.

Following the conference, I dropped off Professor Marion back to Chicago. We attended Mass together on that Sunday evening. I got back into the rental car to drive to Saint Joseph, where I would stay the night at my Mom's. She had been on chemotherapy for ten years and the latest configuration of chemotherapy was beginning to fail. It sounded like there were no other viable alternatives, and I was beginning to feel more and more worried.

I had a voicemail on my cell phone that I listened to before I began driving back to Saint Joseph. It was my Mom, asking me to give her a call when I got back on the road so that she could put a couple of Gino's frozen pizzas into the oven. This was a symbolic food for our family, as it called to mind the treasured memories of going to Chicago for different events while growing up. Chicago deep-dish pizza was a favorite of ours.

What struck me about her gesture was that even though she was undergoing great suffering, she was thinking of me. This is what true mothers do. I got to my Mom's apartment and she gave me a great big hug. I could smell the pizzas baking and I felt at home. She told me that she was beginning to feel pretty weak. I said that I was here for her and would help her out with whatever she needed to be done.

Over the next couple of days, my Mom's health would decline rapidly. I talked with her doctor and the treatment options had run out. After ten years of successful chemo, my Mom's time was up. I had to call in hospice services and they were very supportive. Through their expertise, they were able to help care for my Mom in ways that my brother, Mike, and I were not able to do. At a certain point, I became concerned that my Mom stopped eating and drinking. A hospice nurse reassured me: "Your Mom is dying not because she is not eating and drinking. She is not eating and drinking because she is dying." This was true. My Mom's body was shutting down and her soul was approaching its belated passover. I was in charge of administering morphine moderately to help manage her pain. At one point during the final week of her life, I went out into some woods for a solitary walk in prayer. I brought with me a crucifix that I kept on hand. I remember weeping in the middle of the woods, with the sun illuminating the crucifix in my hands, and saying to God, "Why does it have to be so hard?," as I thought of my Mom's suffering and impending death.

I arrived to my Mom's apartment on Sunday, April 21, 2013. She would go home to be with the Lord in the early hours of the midnight morning, Sunday, April 28. During the last week of my Mom's earthly life, I was reading through Saint John of the Cross's *The Spiritual Canticle*. I read to her the following words of *The Spiritual Canticle* on the evening of Sunday, April 21:

> Since the Israelites were not so fortified in love or so close to God through love, they feared to die upon seeing him. But because now in the law of grace the soul can see God when separated from the body, the desire to live but a short while and die in order to see him is more perfect. And even if this were false, the soul loving God as intensely as this one does would not fear to die from seeing him. True love receives all things that come from the Beloved—prosperity, adversity, even chastisement—with the same evenness of soul, since they are his will. And they afford her joy and delight because, as Saint John says: *Perfect charity casts out all fear* (1 Jn 4:18).
>
> Death cannot be bitter to the soul that loves, for in it she finds all the sweetness and delight of love. The thought of death cannot sadden her, for what she finds is that gladness accompanies this thought. Neither can the thought of death be burdensome and painful to her, for death will put an end to

all her sorrows and afflictions and be the beginning of all her bliss. She thinks of death as her friend and bridegroom, and at the thought of it she rejoices as she would over the thought of her betrothal and marriage, and she longs for the day and the hour of her death more than earthly kings long for kingdoms and principalities.

The Wise Man proclaims of this kind of death: *O death, your sentence is welcome to the person who feels need* (Sirach 41:2). If it is welcome to those who feel need for earthly things, even though it does not provide for these needs but rather despoils such persons of the possessions they have, how much better will its sentence be for the soul in need of love, as is this one crying out for more love. For death will not despoil her of the love she possesses, but rather will be the cause of love's completeness, which she desires, and the satisfaction of all her needs.

The soul is right in daring to say, "may the vision of your beauty be my death," since she knows that at the instant she sees this beauty she will be carried away by it, and absorbed in this very beauty, and transformed in this beauty, and made beautiful like this beauty itself, and enriched and provided for like this very beauty. David declares, consequently, that the death of the saints is precious in the sight of the Lord (Psalm 116:15). This would not be true if they did not participate in God's own grandeurs, for in the sight of God nothing is precious but what he himself is.

Accordingly, the soul does not fear death when she loves; rather she desires it

(Stanza 11.10).

Another verse that stood out from *The Spiritual Canticle* on Thursday of that week, after my Mom had drifted off into a coma, was "that the bride may sleep in deeper peace" (Stanzas 20 and 21.3). My brother, Mike, my Mom's sister, Julie, Jim and Cynda Muldoon, and I were keeping watch with my Mom the night she died. Indeed, she went to sleep in deeper peace in the love of Christ the Bridegroom, at the age of 65.

One of the married couples in my Mom's small Christian community, Jim and Mary Sullivan, distributed prayer cards with the following poem inscribed, on the morning of my Mom's funeral. It was composed by American Discalced Carmelite nun, Jessica Powers, and she entitled it "The Homecoming." The poem ends with the words:

> By naught foretold could she have guessed
> such welcome home: the robe, the ring,

music and endless banqueting,
these people hers; this place of rest
known, as of long remembering
herself a child of God and pressed
with warm endearments to His breast.[1]

I, too, would write a poem about the midnight departure of my Mom and it is published at the end of my 2017 book, *Human and Divine Being: A Study on the Theological Anthropology of Edith Stein*. The poem is entitled "Linda Means Beautiful."

My Mom, Ellen and Tobias.

Uniontown

When my Mom died, my brother, Mike, and I were given inheritance money from our parents' 401K retirement accounts. It was as if our parents were supporting us still from beyond the grave. This money allowed

1. Jessica Powers. *The Selected Poetry of Jessica Powers*. Washington, DC: ICS, 1999, 53.

my family to pursue a new call in life: to move out into the country and live close to the land.

Megan and I found an old modest farmhouse, built in 1906, with twelve acres and several dozens of adjacent acres on which to roam. There also was a gorgeous river that wound around the property. We loved nature, and this property was like living on our very own nature center. It was perfect for our young children to explore and to embark on "a cosmic education," as spoken about by Maria Montessori. We homeschooled all our children, and this was the most idyllic classroom we could have dreamed of. We heated our entire house with wood in the winter and harvested all of the wood from the dead trees of the forest surrounding our house.

Living in Ohio, near Amish country, we caught the horse bug and ended up turning an old garage into two horse stalls. We acquired two horses—a purebred Morgan (named Tenny) and a Pinto quarter horse (named Oscar)—and put up fencing for an outdoor riding arena and pasture. Even though Megan and I did not grow up on a farm or riding horses, our older kids, Ellen and Aubin, participated in some 4-H activities and grew in their interest of horsemanship. We also had Italian honeybees, several barn cats, seven chickens, and even one Betta fish for a while. We would ride the horses on our wooded trails, as well as kayak on inland lakes and reservoirs. It was a most beautiful place, ideal for contemplation and for appreciating the divine genius of creation.

Our new home was in a place called Uniontown. This name had great significance to Megan and me as Secular Discalced Carmelites. We loved to wonder and to wander barefoot in the thick of God's creativity. It was an immaculate place for prayer, especially contemplative prayer. "Uniontown" was a fitting name for the place because it is where our souls were being shaped by the prayer of recollection toward union with the Most Holy Trinity.

A gesture I often would make, even many times daily, was to kiss the palm of my hand and blow kisses to heaven. Every moment was filled with thanksgiving. I spent the whole summer of 2013 mourning my Mom's passing, working like a dog before sunrise to after sunset. The wood my hands handled reminded me of the wood of the cross; the water for the horses and the flowing water of the river reminded me of baptism; the blazing bonfires and the heat of the hearth reminded me of God the Holy Spirit. Everything around me spoke of the paschal mystery, and out in the country you are brought face-to-face with the reality of life and death on a daily basis.

Exploring the world with my children was everything. They taught me to be a child once again. They filled me with an unspeakable joy of being a Dad. They invited me to taste the elemental and be exposed to the earth. I treasure those days with them like a box full of living memories that never grow old. They breathed life into me, just as I breathed life into them. Together we must have "entertained angels" (see Hebrews 13:2).

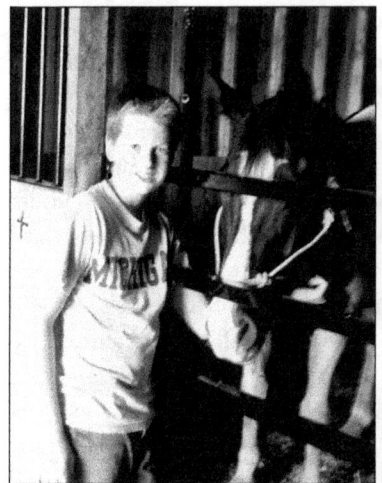

Ellen and Aubin with our horses, Tenny and Oscar.

Fruit of Our Labors

You guessed it: new house, new job, new baby! About nine months after we moved to Uniontown, Oliver Isidore was born. We named him after the Judeo-Christian symbol of the olive branch, a sign of peace, and after Saints Isidore of Seville and Isidore the Farmer.

He was a big boy, and, because labor was induced early, he had some breathing issues right after he was born, since his lungs were not completely developed. He would need to remain in the neo-natal intensive care unit of Akron Children's Hospital for two weeks before coming home to stay. This was another trying time as parents, and we were thankful when he reached full health and could be in the mix of family life.

We now had one girl and five boys. Our home was full of love and vitality. Every day was a new adventure. We both worked hard and played hard. The day was incomplete unless at least one of us got absolutely covered in mud. In many ways we felt like we were in heaven.

The Wallenfang children: Ellen Agnes, Aubin Augustine, Tobias Xavier, Callum Ignatius, Simeon Irenaeus, and Oliver Isidore.

When I was growing up in my family's Higman Park home, I had a toy rocking horse with springs. It sat in the family den, next to the record player. I would rock on that horse for hours every day, rocking to the rhythm of the music. Now we had real horses, and life had come full circle once again. How glorious it is to lead a horse with your children riding above like miniature kings and queens.

Megan, our children and I continued to be active in church life. Megan helped to start up a Catechesis of the Good Shepherd program at Little Flower Parish in Canton. My older children and I helped out with the youth ministry, catechesis, and Matthew 8:20 Ministry, dedicated to feeding the homeless. There were so many families surrounding us who were living out their faith to heroic degrees. We were blessed by their company.

After six years, I had earned the status of tenured professor at Walsh University. This was a lifetime contract and things never felt so secure. It seemed that our family had arrived at everything we had worked for over the years. We became debt-free through lots of discipline and sacrifice, and even our house was paid off. All seemed well and we were enjoying the fruits of our labors nourished by the mercy of God.

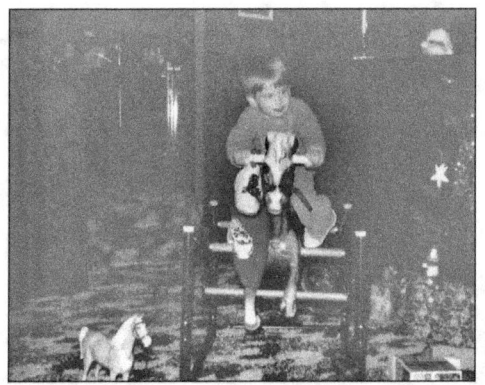

Riding a horse as a child and as an adult.

The Wallenfang family for a candid shot in 2015.

Diabetes

On the feast of Saint Francis of Assisi, October 4, 2016, my daughter, Ellen, at age 15, was diagnosed with juvenile diabetes. She had to stay in the hospital for a week due to dysglycemia, as the disease was discovered late in its onset. This was brand new territory for our family. Quickly we learned all about the disease and the lifestyle adjustments Ellen would have to make to remain healthy.

She had such courage and I was so proud of her. She faced her new circumstances head-on and rolled with the punches. She served as an example to me of what real courage and determination look like. At first, she had to puncture her own skin at least eight times a day, both checking her blood sugar and giving herself injections of insulin. We were thankful that we lived in an era when adequate treatments were available for this disease so that it wouldn't rob her of her life.

I continued to contemplate the meaning of this disease. Diabetes is a wonderful analogy for the spiritual life. Among the meanings of the Greek word, *diabetes*, are "compass" and "to cross over." Diabetes is a health condition which puts you face to face with your limits, and, at the same time, with your possibilities. Living on the threshold between life and death, the antidote for life is always at your side. You have only to receive the injections of a substance that acts as the key to admitting sweetness into all of the cells of your body.

We have what we need to live a resurrection life. The antidote is always at our side: Sacraments, Scripture, fervent prayer, testimonies of the lives of saints, devotions, sacramentals, indulgences, and the mutual support of fellow disciples on the route of faith. We need only to have recourse to the fullness of the antidote and we shall live and be saved.

Locked In

Back in the fall of 2015, I attended an international conference on the work of Edith Stein at the University of Vienna in Austria. I got to stay in the Carmelite monastery in Vienna, as well as the Cistercian abbey in Heiligenkreuz. It was an extraordinary stay, and yet something unusual happened that symbolized so much of what I was experiencing as a young scholar, struggling to be heard and noticed.

On the first evening of the conference that took place at the University of Vienna, the very place where Edmund Husserl had studied mathematics and philosophy, I found myself in a rather unfortunate but humorous predicament.

I had gone to put my luggage in a designated luggage room in the large old academic building. I talked with a couple other scholars in the room and I was the last person remaining in the room after everyone else had exited. I finally went to make my exit and the door was locked! I couldn't get out!

I heard voices on the outside of the room, and I tried knocking on the door to see if anyone would notice. No one did, and I remained locked in the luggage room for the next couple of hours until the keynote presentation in German was finished. Fortunately, I had some good books on hand, but I remember feeling that this odd circumstance reflected how my heart felt in relation to several other scholars who seemed to want to box me out of the club for whatever reason.

Beethoven 7

Prior to my trip to the Stein conference in Vienna, I searched the website of the Vienna Philharmonic Orchestra to find out if they were performing any concerts during the days that I would be in town. My father's favorite classical piece of music was Ludwig von Beethoven's 7th Symphony. And what was the Vienna Philharmonic scheduled to perform when I was in town? You guessed it: Beethoven 7 (and 8)! I could not believe this state of affairs!

The only problem was that this performance was for season ticket holders only. I still had to email the box office to find out if there was any way for me to purchase a ticket to this concert. A nice gentleman said that there was a chance that a patron might not be able to make the show, and, in that case, I would be able to purchase that ticket.

So, what happened? Sure enough, a seat came available: third row middle! As my Mom used to say, "You live a charmed life, kid! A charmed life!" I gladly purchased the ticket and incredibly enjoyed the performance. Beethoven Symphony 8 was played first, followed by Symphony 7. I felt as though on the threshold of heaven. At intermission I enjoyed a Coke and some delicious Austrian pastries. *Genuß*! During the middle of the 7th Symphony, a phrase came to mind: "A passion beyond passion." This is what I was experiencing. An enjoyment beyond base lustful enjoyments that prevent the soul from soaring among the heights of divine glory. "Do not love the world or the things of the world. If anyone loves the world, the love of the Father is not in him. For all that is in the world, the lust of the flesh, the lust of the eyes, and the pride of life, is not from the Father but is from the world. Yet the world and its enticement are passing away. But whoever does the will of God remains forever" (1 John 2:15–17).

Rendezvous with Destiny—Part II

Earlier in this book, I told the story of how I applied to the University of Notre Dame and was not admitted. The door had remained closed. Yet, after meeting Dr. John Cavadini at the Edith Stein conference at Notre Dame, he became an incredibly supportive friend, mentor and colleague. I was not worthy of his support, yet, for whatever reason, he saw something in me that perhaps I didn't even see in myself.

I was having difficulty finding a publisher for my first two books. They were "too Catholic" for the more secular-oriented presses and "too philosophical" for the more religious-oriented presses. I felt like a homeless author with nowhere to turn. Dr. Cavadini agreed to meet with me at his office after having a look at my manuscripts.

I arrived at Geddes Hall on the hallowed campus of my childhood dreams. Dr. Cavadini welcomed me with fatherly care. I was surprised to find out that he had underwent a colonoscopy procedure that morning! He didn't want to cancel his appointment with me, so he kept it and quietly suffered through his discomfort to meet with me graciously and warmly.

He told me that my writing reminded him of that of Origen of Alexandria, one of his favorite patristic authors, and that he found it beautiful. He said that he was convinced that it was worthy of publication and it was just a matter of time until I found the right home for the texts. He would endorse the works and help in any way to see them through to publication.

Later on, I had a dream within a dream in which Dr. Cavadini made an appearance. In this dream I was talking with Dr. Cavadini on the campus of Notre Dame. In the dream, I told him that I had a dream and he spoke to me in my dream. Dr. Cavadini asked me, "And what did I say to you in your dream?" And I replied to him, "You spoke positively of my work."

To make a long story short, my books found a happy home with Wipf and Stock Publishers. They were a trending ecumenical press out of Eugene, Oregon, and their publishing culture let authors be themselves. You didn't have to pretend or conform to some ideological platform, thereby watering down the fullness of your written voice or scholarship.

Dr. Cavadini ended up writing a complimentary foreword to my book on the work of Edith Stein, and Dr. Cyril O'Regan, also from the University of Notre Dame, wrote an endorsement for the back cover. Dr. Cavadini also wrote an endorsement for the back cover of my book on the Eucharist, and Jean-Luc Marion wrote the foreword.

John Cavadini and I would go on to create and co-edit a book series called *Global Perspectives on the New Evangelization*. He later would host me as a guest speaker at a conference sponsored by the Institute for Church Life at Notre Dame, on the work of Joseph Ratzinger. On the morning of my presentation in McKenna Hall, I stepped outside the building for some fresh air and thanksgiving right before it was about to begin. There was a flock of migrating birds filling the tree outside the building, singing away with reference to their Creator. I was about to sing his praises too, appearing on campus as a hidden underdog witness to what the power of God can do.

It is wonderfully ironic that Dr. Cavadini became chair of the theology department at the University of Notre Dame the very year that I was denied admission to the school. Now he was writing a foreword and endorsement for my own books! Better than a Heisman trophy, better than a national championship, better than "Touchdown Jesus" facing me, these books pointed to him. All that happened through Jesus was the real touchdown and victory. It wasn't all about me after all. iGod inverted.

In my hotel room of the Morris Inn for the Ratzinger conference at the University of Notre Dame in the fall of 2018.

Kidney

The year after I had been hired at Walsh University, our theology department was able to hire another theology faculty member. His name was Andrew ("Drew") Kim. He did his doctorate at the Catholic University of America and was a very intelligent and relevant young Catholic moral scholar. The other theology faculty members and I were very impressed with his interview, and he got the job offer, hands down.

Drew was married to Caitlin and they had several young children. Shortly after he began working at Walsh, Drew made a shocking announcement at one of our theology faculty meetings. During their present pregnancy, it was discovered that his wife, Caitlin, was born with only one kidney and that her kidney was beginning to fail. My heart immediately went out to Drew and his family and I couldn't imagine what it would be like to be in that situation.

Drew of course went through the necessary tests to determine if he could be a kidney donor for his wife. It turned out that he had kidney stones, and, therefore, was disqualified as a potential donor. I was continuing to study and teach the works of Emmanuel Levinas, as well as grow in my Catholic faith. The theme of both Levinas's work, and the life of Jesus Christ, is responsibility for the other. I gave this theme lip service all the time, but now was confronted with a real dilemma. Caitlin had O-positive blood. I had O-positive blood and would donate this blood frequently. After talking things over with Megan, we both were resolved about the next move to make.

One afternoon in the undercroft of the chapel at Walsh, I walked across the hall to the office of my colleague, Drew. In the short time he had been at Walsh, he and I were known for getting into quite heated theological debates. He tended to come at things from a more metaphysical standpoint, and I came at them from a more phenomenological angle. We didn't always see eye-to-eye, but, nevertheless, we had deep respect for each other.

That afternoon, I entered Drew's office and asked if it would be alright for me to get tested to find out if I could be a potential kidney donor for Caitlin. He said sure and sent me the contact info for their kidney donor coordinator at the Cleveland Clinic. I went through all the tests and it turned out that I was the perfect donor.

Suddenly nearing a time to schedule the transplant surgery, it turned out that Caitlin became pregnant. The surgery would need to wait until a future date, while in the meantime Caitlin's uterus helped to act as a kind of second kidney during pregnancy.

Within the next year, Drew ended up accepting a new position as a faculty member at Marquette University in Milwaukee, Wisconsin. I told him that I always would be willing to donate my kidney to Caitlin, even out of state. After their new baby, Olivia, was born, I had to go through the entire round of testing again. All turned out well, and I was cleared to be the perfect donor once again, this time through the University of Wisconsin Organ Transplant Program.

In March of 2019, I made a stay in Denver, Colorado, as I presented a seminar on evangelization at the Saint John Institute. The day before my flight was supposed to leave to travel back to Ohio, a blizzard swept through the area. My flight was cancelled, and I had to stay in the Denver area for an additional couple of days. I ended up driving out to Estes Park for a quiet personal retreat. It was a breathtaking place (at times quite literally!) and I wanted to climb a mountain.

I had only my dress shoes and dress clothes, but I was intent on this adventure. Near Camp Saint Malo, a place Saint John Paul II visited back in 1993, I found the perfect snow-covered mountain to climb: Lily Mountain. With bear spray in hand, I ascended the mountain, step by step by step. While climbing, I thought about giving up my kidney. It scared me a bit, just like climbing an unknown mountain. But the words that kept echoing in my head as a spiritual refrain were those of Blessed Pier Giorgio Frassati: *Verso l'alto* ("To the top!"). By the grace of God, I made it to the top of that mountain and back down in solitude. It was an amazing peak and showcased the grandeur of God's creation.

On the way down the mountain, a mother, father and young adult son were making their ascent. I was sitting down in the snow, trying to warm my feet temporarily because I was having trouble feeling them. The father of the family had a Wisconsin Badgers sweatshirt on. I told them that I wasn't crazy, just an ignorant tourist from Ohio who forgot to bring proper footwear. We exchanged greetings and I learned that they were from Madison, Wisconsin. I ended up telling them that I would be donating a kidney to someone there later that year. They wished me the best and continued to ascend the mountain.

Later, as the donor, I got to pick the date for the surgery. I chose May 1, 2019, as it was the feast day of Saint Joseph the Worker. As I understood it, I would be going to work that day through an active passivity of self-donation. One of my kidneys was no longer mine. It was hers, and Caitlin had a claim on it inasmuch as she was in desperate need of it. As I contemplated the meaning of this kidney donation, it seemed like it would be, as a man, the closest thing to giving birth. The very procedure would involve removing the kidney from my body, right below my navel. To give birth is to grant life to an other-than-the-self.

A few months before the surgery took place, I had to travel to Madison to complete a new round of tests. I stayed overnight at the Kim's home that trip, and we had a wonderful time together. Drew and I ate dinner at the perfect Italian restaurant, across the street from the UW Hospital, Lombardino's, reminiscent (to me) of the great Green Bay Packers's coach, Vince Lombardi. There was something of victory and celebration in the air, even preveniently. Getting to be in the Kim's home to contemplate their family life, their six beautiful children, and all that it would mean for Caitlin to be restored to health was a tremendous gift and inspiration to me. I truly was saturated by the beauty of their family, and I knew that giving up my kidney would grant greater life to all of them. When I was saying goodbye and about to leave to travel back to Ohio, one of their daughter's, Phoebe, said to me, "I want you to stay here forever!" I thought to myself,

"In a way, I will be remaining with you and your family forever, through a presence of absence in the form of a kidney."

Leading up to the date of the transplant surgery, I found myself being drawn to watch many mountain climbing videos on YouTube. Mount Everest, K2, the Swiss Alps. I even ended up posting my own humble summit experience of Lily Mountain on YouTube as well! For me, approaching donating my kidney was like ascending a mountain with daring and boldness, relying on the strength that only God supplies. It required bracketing fear (even though it did not cease to threaten), and moving toward the summit, one step at a time.

After many further preparatory tests and blood draws, May 1, 2019 came. The night before the surgery, I had to shower and rub a couple of disinfecting solutions all over my body. It was a bit surreal, preparing my own body to become a more concrete gift of itself. May 1 was a very gloomy day—dismal, cold and rainy. Megan and I entered the hospital and worked our way to the organ donation unit. I felt quite nervous. This was real. Even the remote possibility of dying today was real.

Alongside the "First Day Surgery" waiting room was a large mural of a mountain, and the perspective presented in the picture was as if you were looking out from the summit of the mountain. It filled the entire wall. This scene spoke volumes to me all at once, as it signified the very destination at which I had arrived that morning. I was so nervous that I had to urinate over a dozen times before going into surgery.

Eventually my name was called as I sat in the waiting room. Here we go. I was escorted to surgery prep room #3—again symbolic of the football number I wore in high school and in college, symbolic of the signal my Dad would give to my Mom growing up (three fingers in the air, meaning, "I love you"), symbolic of the Most Holy Trinity who gave me life and taught me that in order to save my life I must lose it (see Matthew 16:25).

Dr. Luis Fernandez of Venezuela would be performing the surgery. The entire team of doctors and nurses was very warm and joyful. I received a kiss from Megan as I was wheeled toward the operating room. I was fully conscious and one of the anesthesiologists asked if I wanted to take some pills that would make me rather drowsy and relieve any anxiety. I declined, as I wanted to near this summit fully willing, conscious and aware.

Once in the operating room, I was asked to transfer myself to the operating table and then to extend my right arm straight out, across a table extension, beginning to make a cruciform shape. I understood what was happening to be, in some mysterious way, a participation in what Jesus went through on Mount Golgotha. All was joy and gift.

Next, I awoke in a dark recovery room with two nurses attending to me. Praise and thanksgiving to God immediately issued from my lips in a whisper. I was alive! There were five wounds on my body: four laparoscopic incisions in the shape of a cross on my left abdomen and one large incision beneath my navel. I was transferred to another room and was met by Megan and Drew. They had talked with the surgeon and it sounded like all had gone well, though the surgery lasted considerably longer than anticipated, by several hours. The surgeon said that I had "a complicated anatomy."

It is interesting to discover that, in Hebrew idiom, the kidneys refer to the seat of conscience and serve as a metaphor of the inner moral life of a person. Several biblical texts indicate that God searches and tests "the kidneys" ("mind/heart"; see Psalms 7:10; 26:2; Revelation 2:23). Also, we find that Torah prescribes that the kidneys of animals be offered as holocausts before the Lord (see Leviticus 3:4, 10, 15). "Aaron's sons shall burn this on the altar with the burnt offering that is on the wood and the embers, as a sweet-smelling oblation to the LORD" (Leviticus 3:5). Another biblical passage that intrigues me is Psalm 16:7: "My reins ("kidneys") also instruct me in the night seasons" (King James Version). Through the duration of the dark night of the soul (Saint John of the Cross), the kidneys are there to instruct us. Just as there is a devotion to the Sacred Heart of Jesus, perhaps here we find cause to introduce a new devotion to the Sacred Kidneys of Jesus. May he never fail to instruct us by his Sacred Heart and Kidneys throughout our sojourn of this mountain of life.

Caitlin Kim and I the day after the kidney transplant surgery.

I Love Your Church, O Lord

My recovery following the transplant surgery went very well. I would leave from the hospital the day after the surgery took place. We were driving back home to Ohio and Megan told me about a job opening she had seen online: a full-time faculty position at Sacred Heart Major Seminary in Detroit, Michigan. I had heard great things about the place and the New Evangelization movement in the Archdiocese of Detroit. I was animated to apply for the position and did so the day after we arrived home.

Upon arriving home, I got out of the rental suburban with great thanksgiving. I took a walk by myself toward the back of our property, thinking about the mystery of the surgery and this new job possibility as a seminary professor. I prayed these words out loud: "I love your Church, O Lord." I began to envision that this might be a new call from God to go to Detroit. I had not yet applied for the position, but an assurance welled up in me that confirmed the destination in advance. I called upon the intercession of many saints, including the recently deceased African American Pentecostal-pastor-turned-Catholic-deacon from Detroit, Alex Jones, as well as recently beatified Capuchin friar, Blessed Solanus Casey, who served in ministry for twenty years at Saint Bonaventure convent in Detroit, and died at a Detroit hospital in 1957.

Why was I on the hunt for a new faculty position? The liberal arts were being eroded at Walsh University and even tenured faculty were being let go. The threat of eliminating majors began to be aimed at history, literature, music, philosophy and theology, and I had to do due diligence in applying to some other open positions. This was a difficult time, but Megan and I trusted that divine providence would see us through this storm once again. An encouraging word came to me in prayer: "I do not know what the future holds, but I know who holds the future."

Piccolo Mondo

Following the transplant surgery, later on that same month of May, my family and I travelled to the Upper Peninsula of Michigan to visit Megan's parents. We would stop in Chicago en route, to visit Megan's sister, Natalie, and for me to get a chance to sit in on one of Professor Marion's lectures and to go out to dinner with him. Professor Marion recommended that we eat at a local Italian restaurant called Piccolo Mondo ("small world").

After his lecture, I met he and his wife, Corinne, at the restaurant for a brilliant dinner and conversation. One of the questions I asked him had to do with his experience of relative fame. He said to me with a smile, "It's not real."

Upon finishing our meal, we walked outside to meet Megan and our children in our minivan. This was the first time that Professor Marion and his wife met them. Professor Marion peeked his head in at my children and said to them, "Your father is a great philosopher!" That was more than generous of him to say, but, at the same time, it was an encouraging word of affirmation.

As another full circle moment, I couldn't help but give thanks to God for bringing me to this point. Looking back, I don't know how else I could have arrived here apart from his grace and undeserved open doors by his unsuspecting hand. It was a small world after all.

Late-Morning Locution

On June 25, 2019, I ate lunch outdoors at Bam! Restaurant, across the street from Walsh University, on a vivid summer day. It was around 11:00AM. The food there was sensational, and I was busy contemplating the goodness of many things, above all, the goodness of God. Saint Augustine's *Confessions* was sitting on the table in front of me next to a cup of water and an empty dish.

All of a sudden, I heard a female voice behind me, sounding like it came from a loud car stereo passing by, saying: "Speak the truth, even if it leads to your death." The sound faded out immediately as the word "death" was being uttered. I turned around and saw no vehicle but only felt the gentle breeze spreading over me and the potted flowers.

Detroit

After video and on-campus interviews, and lots of waiting, on July 2, 2019, I received a phone call from Fr. Timothy Laboe, the Dean of Studies at Sacred Heart Major Seminary. I had made my on-campus interview there on the feast of the Sacred Heart of Jesus. He offered me the position as full professor of theology and philosophy. After some negotiation, I accepted the position and my family prepared ourselves for yet another move to foreign territory, although back to our home state.

The French name, Detroit, means "a strait," that is, a narrow and constricted passageway. It calls to mind the words of Jesus in the gospel: "Enter through the narrow gate; for the gate is wide and the road broad that leads to destruction, and those who enter through it are many. How narrow the gate and constricted the road that leads to life. And those who find it are few" (Matthew 7:13-14).

I knew that Detroit was one of the poorest and most run-down cities in the United States. It was a land of "greyfield" and desolation, but, at the same time, I knew that this is precisely the place where God the Holy Spirit wants to be at work. I also knew that the Holy Spirit already was at work there and that Detroit was inherently rich in ethnic diversity and a crossroads of the great religious traditions of the world. I was excited to be a part of the mission of the Church in this place, and my family and I would trade in our horses and settled life for another missionary adventure. We would pack up our contemplative Carmelite apostolate and relocate to an island outside the city—a land called Harsens Island, betwixt the North and South Channels of the Saint Clair River. Saint Clair (from the French spelling of Saint Clare of Assisi) herself was a contemplative nun and we felt right at home, surrounded by these contemplative waters.

And so, a richly diverse and vibrantly alive city lives on, even through this perilous time of the Coronavirus that has hit Detroit so hard over the springtime of 2020. "See what love the Father has bestowed on us that we may be called the children of God. Yet so we are. The reason the world does not know us is that it did not know him. Beloved, we are God's children now; what we shall be has not yet been revealed. We do know that when it is revealed we shall be like him, for we shall see him as he is. Everyone who has this hope based on him makes himself pure, as he is pure" (1 John 3:1-3).

The Wallenfang family outside our Harsens Island home in the late fall of 2019.

Strength in Suffering

There was a man I noticed on Harsens Island who appeared to have cerebral palsy or some other similarly related disability. When riding my bike past his home, I would see him moving slowly about, sometimes walking his dog. Seeing him always drew my attention back to God and the words the Lord spoke to Saint Paul: "My grace is sufficient for you, for power is made perfect in weakness" (2 Cor 12:9).

Our first few months in our new home were trying ones, due to a variety of reasons. Suffice it to say that we were having a tough run trying to get resettled and adjusting to the new set of conditions and Motown lifestyle. Some powerful verses in Scripture illustrate both the trial and glimmer of hope we were experiencing at the time:

> So humble yourselves under the mighty hand of God, that he may exalt you in due time. Cast all your worries upon him because he cares for you. Be sober and vigilant. Your opponent the devil is prowling around like a roaring lion looking for someone to devour. Resist him, steadfast in faith, knowing that your

fellow believers throughout the world undergo the same sufferings. The God of all grace who called you to his eternal glory through Christ Jesus will himself restore, confirm, strengthen, and establish you after you have suffered a little. To him be dominion forever. Amen (1 Peter 5:6–11).

Sometime in February of 2020, Megan and I were taking a walk one afternoon passed this enigmatic man's home, as mentioned above. Later I would meet him personally and discovered that his name was Jim. There he was, walking his dog toward us with a great big smile on his face. As he passed by, I said, "Hello, how are you?" And he turned around, he looked at us with that radiant smile, and replied, "Everything is marvelous!"

Silhouettes of my children and I on the shore of Lake Michigan where I was raised. This picture was taken on April 29, 2013, the day after my mother's passing into eternal life. Seagulls soared before the setting sun.

"Accent on the Offbeat"
The name of God is mercy, this we know for sure.
If he held not the antidote, without a doubt no cure.
Since he is Judge, at once he must be Healer, Mender, Pure.
For only God with scale and nail and ~~strikethrough~~ can allure.
Without your Cross, I am lost, a nomad, nihil dicit.
With your Blood, I am your bud, "Blossòm," Domìnus dixit.
Jesus Christ, whose Name is Love, a Hero and an Athlete.
More sonorous than any song, with accent on the Offbeat.

Holy Spirit, dare I take your Wind within my sail?
Where might you push me, pull me, will it not be in travail?
The word out on the street is that you are a mighty Gale.
Do I resist or let you in? How else to catch the whale?

The Wallenfang family inside our Harsens Island home in the early fall of 2020.

INDEX

Abraham, 165–66
adulthood, 29
Albion, 83–84, 86, 91–94, 99–100, 103–15, 123–25, 133, 137, 177
Aquinas, Thomas. *See* Thomas Aquinas.
Augustine of Hippo, 174, 181, 203

baptism, 11, 14, 141, 156, 189
beauty, 34, 97, 109, 121, 139, 153, 175, 187, 199
Blue Lake Fine Arts Camp, 46–47, 49, 94

Carmelite (or Carmelites), 174, 184–85, 187, 189, 194, 204
Catholicism, 132
Cavadini, John, 174, 195–96
Chicago, 59, 156, 158, 160–63, 166, 169–171, 185, 202
childhood, 8, 11, 29, 79, 101, 141, 195
confession, 164–65
conscience, 48, 165, 201
contemplation, 109, 121, 189
conversation (or conversations), 22, 30, 45, 56, 80, 99–100, 109, 113, 133, 171–72, 185, 202
conversion, ix–x, 32, 92, 95, 153, 164
Creator, 137, 196
culture (or cultures), 108, 172, 176, 179, 181, 196

Detroit, 59, 85, 202–204
diabetes, 193

ethics, 156, 168
Eucharist, 119, 138, 153, 164, 168, 171, 196
evangelization, 196, 198, 202
evil, 63, 178, 181

father (or fatherhood, fathers, grandfather), x, 6, 10, 38, 45–46, 55, 59, 73, 87, 111, 118, 123, 128, 130, 135, 137–39, 142–44, 146–48, 151, 164, 170, 176–77, 182, 194–95, 199, 203–204
forgiveness, 184
Francis of Assisi, 193
Francis Xavier, 151, 166
Franciscan University of Steubenville, 119
Franklin, Kirk, 105

glory, 50, 60, 66, 92, 107, 120, 127, 137, 140, 149, 161, 164, 195, 206
goodness, 27, 55, 88, 96, 121, 153, 171, 175, 203
Gospel, 93, 95, 105, 107, 111, 130, 153, 156, 177, 203
grace, 59, 138, 150–51, 153, 164, 167, 171, 186, 199, 203, 205–206
Green Bay Packers, 75, 146, 199

Heartmenders, 5–6
hell, 8, 18, 60, 68
Higman Park, 1–4, 7, 18, 34, 38, 108, 117, 137, 191
Holocaust (or holocausts), 168, 180, 201
Holy Spirit, x, 123, 138–39, 151–53, 156, 164, 166, 189, 204, 207
hope (or hoped, hopeful, hopefully, hopes), ix–x, 2–3, 8, 20, 30, 41, 64, 72, 78, 80, 82–83, 85–88, 92, 97, 99, 106, 124–126, 143, 149, 155, 164–65, 167, 176–77, 182, 204–205

intellectual, 27, 72
interpretation, 68, 94
interreligious dialogue, 3, 5, 23, 31–32, 39, 43, 61n

jazz, 27, 73, 102–103, 107, 109–10, 113, 120, 138
Jesus of Nazareth, 9, 55, 74–75, 95, 105, 118–19, 123, 128, 138, 144, 150, 152–53, 164–65, 179, 196, 198, 200–201, 203, 206
Jewish, 168, 174, 179–80
John of the Cross, 184, 186, 201
John Paul II, Pope, 135–36, 184, 199
Johnson, James Weldon, 182

Kalamazoo, 1, 10, 99, 122, 124, 128–29, 135, 137, 140, 176
kidney (or kidneys), 197–201
King, Martin Luther, 180–81

Lake Michigan Catholic, 24, 30, 33, 38, 51, 91, 142
law, 180–81, 186
liturgy, 12, 128, 130, 133, 150, 163
Levinas, Emmanuel, 1, 168, 179–80, 198
Loyola University Chicago, 156–62, 165–70, 173

Madonna Della Strada Chapel, 165–66
Marion, Jean-Luc, 160–63, 168–71, 185, 196, 202–203
Marsalis, Wynton, 72–73, 107, 114
Mary of Nazareth, 99, 128, 165

ministry (or ministries), 104–105, 113, 118, 128, 133–34, 137–39, 143, 149–56, 163, 177, 182, 192, 202
Montana, Joe, 22, 88
mother (or motherhood, mothers, grandmother), 1, 3, 8, 10, 43, 45–46, 115, 133, 135, 139, 144, 159, 165–66, 169, 176–77, 185, 199, 206
Mount Carmel, 139
mystical (or mystic), 95–96, 124, 146, 162

Niagara, 14, 28, 142

peace (or peaceful, peacefully), 16, 27, 30, 55, 63, 69, 86, 152, 166, 187, 190
phenomenology, 160, 163, 168–69, 185
philosophy, 160, 168, 174, 180, 185, 194, 202–203
political, 8, 44, 175, 177–78
poverty, 97
Promise Keepers, 59, 99
prophet, 152, 177–78
Protestant, 54, 104, 122, 131–32

Rahner, Karl, 152, 156
reconciliation, 60, 150
Reeperbahn, 46–47
resurrection, 123, 164, 194

sacrament (or sacramental, sacramentals, sacraments), 118–19, 130, 135, 147, 164, 194
Sacred Heart, 74, 201–203
Saint Augustine Cathedral, 120, 125, 128–29, 133
Saint Ignace, 111
Saint Norbert College, 150–52, 160
Scripture (or Scriptures), 56, 93, 96, 99, 119, 132, 152, 194, 205
Shakespeare, 56–57
soul (or souls), 8, 27, 37, 44, 59, 96–97, 101–102, 109, 125–26, 138, 143, 148–49, 163–64, 167, 169, 184, 186–87, 189, 195, 201

spirit (or spirits, spiritual, spirituality), x, 75, 96, 99, 102, 113, 123, 138–39, 151–53, 156, 164, 166, 170, 173, 184, 186–87, 189, 193, 199, 204, 207
Stein, Edith (or Teresa Benedicta of the Cross), 173–74, 184, 194–96

Teresa of Ávila, 184
Thomas Aquinas, 166
Torah, 201
transcendence, 135

universal, 174

Urbana Conference, 94–96, 126

Victory Park, 102, 123–25
vocation, 58–59, 130, 135, 139–40, 150, 157, 173, 181

Waffle House, 49–50
Walsh University, 174–75, 185, 192, 197–98, 202–203
Western Michigan University, 61, 114–15, 120–22, 126, 132–33, 138, 143
wisdom, 12, 27, 39, 65, 82, 100, 116, 181

www.ingramcontent.com/pod-product-compliance
Lightning Source LLC
Chambersburg PA
CBHW070322230426
43663CB00011B/2193